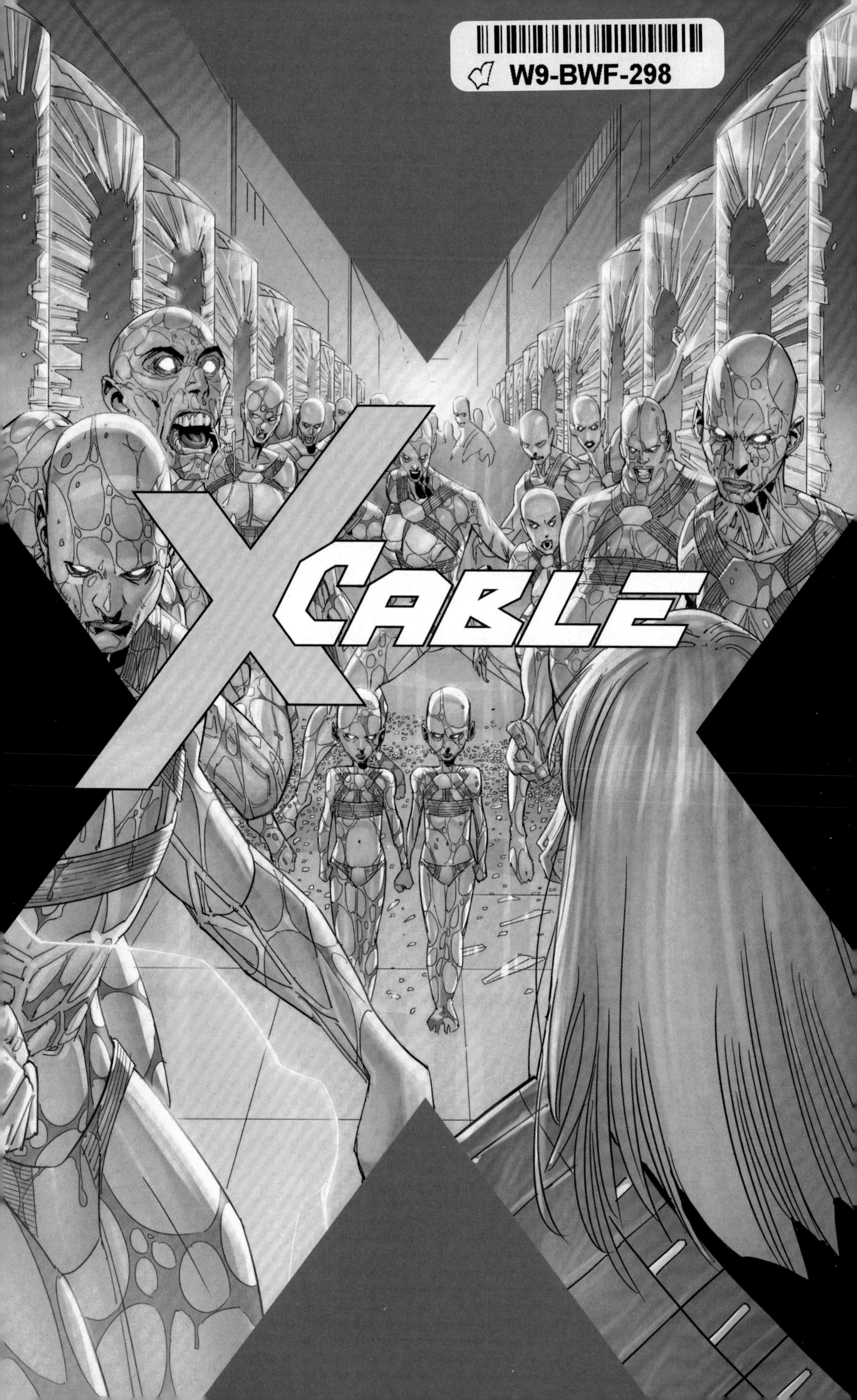

X
CABLE

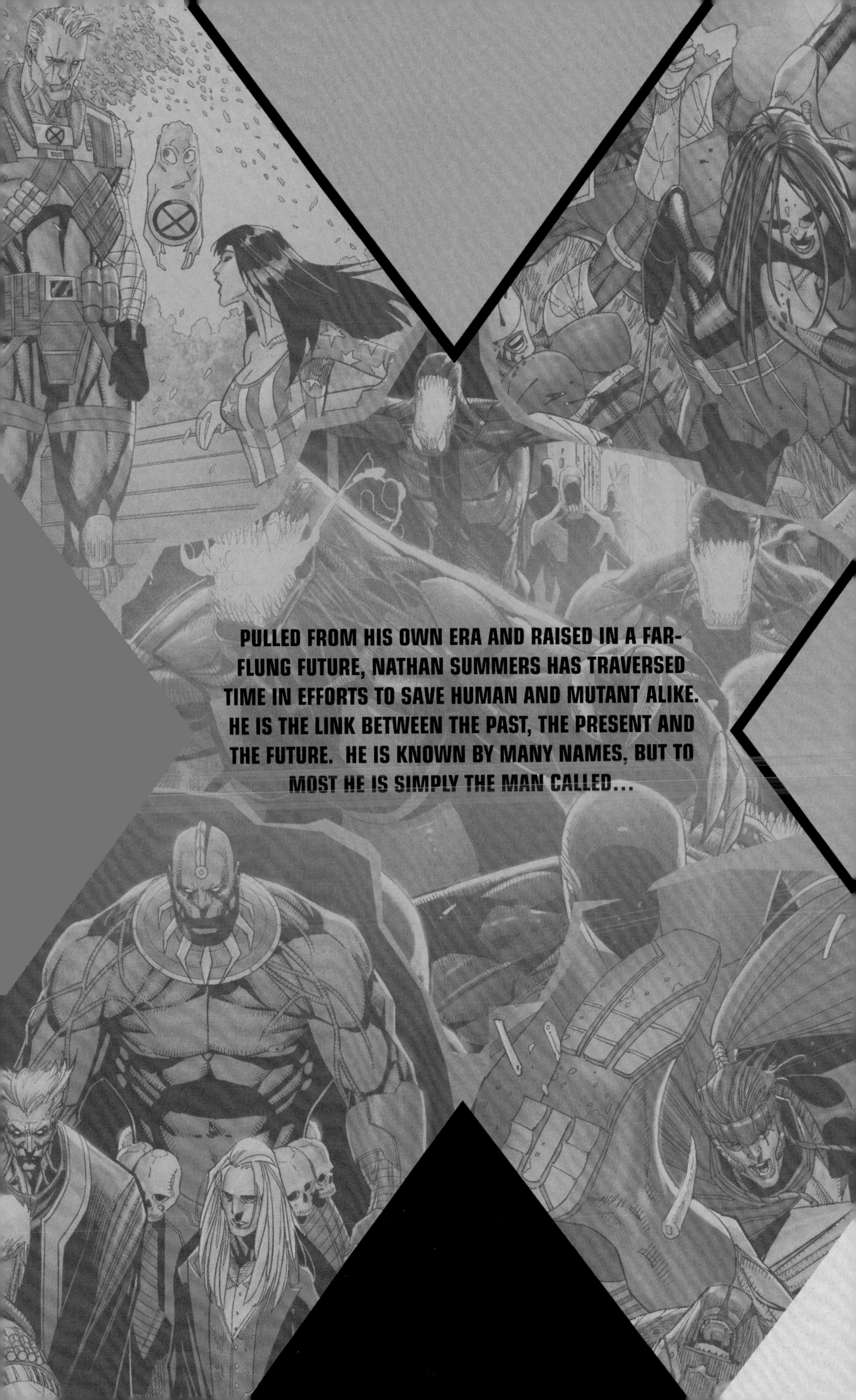
PULLED FROM HIS OWN ERA AND RAISED IN A FAR-FLUNG FUTURE, NATHAN SUMMERS HAS TRAVERSED TIME IN EFFORTS TO SAVE HUMAN AND MUTANT ALIKE. HE IS THE LINK BETWEEN THE PAST, THE PRESENT AND THE FUTURE. HE IS KNOWN BY MANY NAMES, BUT TO MOST HE IS SIMPLY THE MAN CALLED...

THE NEWER MUTANTS

Writer/**ED BRISSON**

Artist/**JON MALIN**
Color Artist/**JESUS ABURTOV**
with **FEDERICO BLEE** (#154)

Letterer/**VC's TRAVIS LANHAM**
Cover Art/**JON MALIN**
& **FEDERICO BLEE**

Assistant Editor/**CHRIS ROBINSON**
Associate Editor/**MARK BASSO**
Editor/**DARREN SHAN**
X-Men Group Editor/**MARK PANICCIA**

Collection Editor/**JENNIFER GRÜNWALD** • Assistant Editor/**CAITLIN O'CONNELL**
Associate Managing Editor/**KATERI WOODY** • Editor, Special Projects/**MARK D. BEAZLEY**
VP Production & Special Projects/**JEFF YOUNGQUIST** • SVP Print, Sales & Marketing/**DAVID GABRIEL**
Book Designer/**JAY BOWEN**

Editor in Chief/**C.B. CEBULSKI** • Chief Creative Officer/**JOE QUESADA**
President/**DAN BUCKLEY** • Executive Producer/**ALAN FINE**

CABLE VOL. 2: THE NEWER MUTANTS. Contains material originally published in magazine form as CABLE #150-154. First printing 2018. ISBN 978-1-302-90483-8. Published by MARVEL WORLDWIDE, INC., a subsidiary of MARVEL ENTERTAINMENT, LLC. OFFICE OF PUBLICATION: 135 West 50th Street, New York, NY 10020. **Printed in Canada.** DAN BUCKLEY, President, Marvel Entertainment; JOHN NEE, Publisher; JOE QUESADA, Chief Creative Officer; TOM BREVOORT, SVP of Publishing; DAVID BOGART, SVP of Business Affairs & Operations, Publishing & Partnership; DAVID GABRIEL, SVP of Sales & Marketing, Publishing; JEFF YOUNGQUIST, VP of Production & Special Projects; DAN CARR, Executive Director of Publishing Technology; ALEX MORALES, Director of Publishing Operations; SUSAN CRESPI, Production Manager; STAN LEE, Chairman Emeritus. For information regarding advertising in Marvel Comics or on Marvel.com, please contact Vit DeBellis, Custom Solutions & Integrated Advertising Manager, at vdebellis@marvel.com. For Marvel subscription inquiries, please call 888-511-5480. **Manufactured between 2/16/2018 and 3/20/2018 by SOLISCO PRINTERS, SCOTT, QC, CANADA.**

10 9 8 7 6 5 4 3 2 1

150

NEW ORLEANS.
13 YEARS AGO.
NEW ORLEANS FORENSIC CENTER
WHEN ARE YOU LIVING THESE DAYS? WHERE YOU CALLING HOME?
A FEW YEARS FROM NOW, DOESN'T MATTER WHEN.
MORGUE
OH YEAH? WHAT'S IT LIKE "A FEW YEARS FROM NOW"? WHAT'S CHANGED?
KLANK
RGUE
NOT A WHOLE LOT.
PHONES GOT SMALLER, THEN BIGGER AGAIN.
YOU KNOW, EVERY TIME YOU SEE A CORONER WORKING OVER A BODY ON TV, THEY'RE STUFFING FOOD INTO THEIR FACE.
ALWAYS WONDERED IF THAT WERE TRUE.
IS IT?
HEY! THIS IS A CLOSED--
WHAT?

DO YOU EAT SANDWICHES OVER THE BODIES WHILE YOU DO THE AUTOPSIES?
WHAT? NO! THAT'S...
WHO **ARE** YOU PEOPLE?
GET OUT.
WE NEED THE ROOM FOR FIFTEEN MINUTES.
NO.
YOU **CAN'T** BE IN HERE. YOU--
YOU SEE THAT GUN STRAPPED TO MY BACK?
THE... GUN?
IT'S BIG. **HARD** TO MISS.
THE GUN MEANS WE CAN BE IN HERE.
THERE'S A CHAIR OUTSIDE...
...TAKE A SEAT.

WOW.
MANNERS NOT A THING IN THE FUTURE?
I DON'T NEED A LECTURE ON ETIQUETTE.
I NEED YOUR **HELP.**
FOLLOWED A TIME ANOMALY HERE TO NEW ORLEANS BUT THE TRAIL WENT COLD BEFORE I COULD ZERO IN ON WHO.
KA-CHUNK
I DON'T BELIEVE IT'S JUST A COINCIDENCE THAT A FEW HOURS LATER, **SHE** TURNS UP DEAD.
BROUGHT IN AS A JANE DOE. FINGERPRINTS, DENTAL, BLOODWORK...NO MATCH TO ANY OF IT.
ON PAPER, SHE DOESN'T EXIST.
YOU KNOW HER?
HER NAME IS CANDRA.
AN EXTERNAL. MEMBER OF BOTH THE THIEVES GUILD **AND** ASSASSINS GUILD. SHE'S **SUPPOSED** TO BE IMMORTAL.
DOESN'T BEING DEAD SORT OF NEGATE THAT?

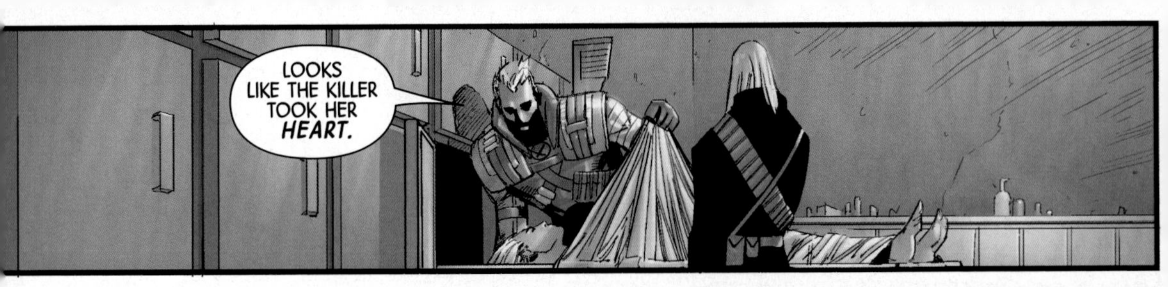
LOOKS LIKE THE KILLER TOOK HER **HEART.**

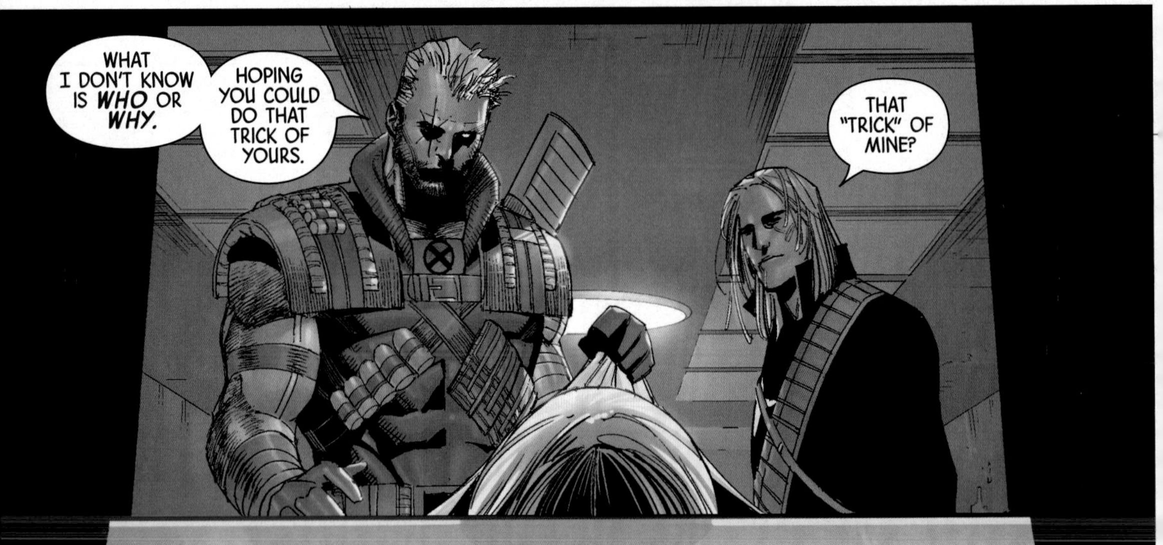
WHAT I DON'T KNOW IS **WHO** OR **WHY.**
HOPING YOU COULD DO THAT TRICK OF YOURS.
THAT "TRICK" OF MINE?

OKAY, OKAY.
BUT, I'VE GOT TO WARN YOU...
NORMALLY, THIS ONLY WORKS ON THE RECENTLY DECEA--
WHOA!

"SHE WAS SLEEPING...
"SOMETHING WOKE HER UP.

"IT'S...SOMEONE'S THERE TO KILL HER. AN OLD FRIEND?
"CAN'T MAKE OUT A FACE. NOT EVEN A SILHOUETTE. BUT SHE KNOWS THEM. SHE'S SURPRISED TO SEE THEM.

"SHE PUT UP A FIGHT.

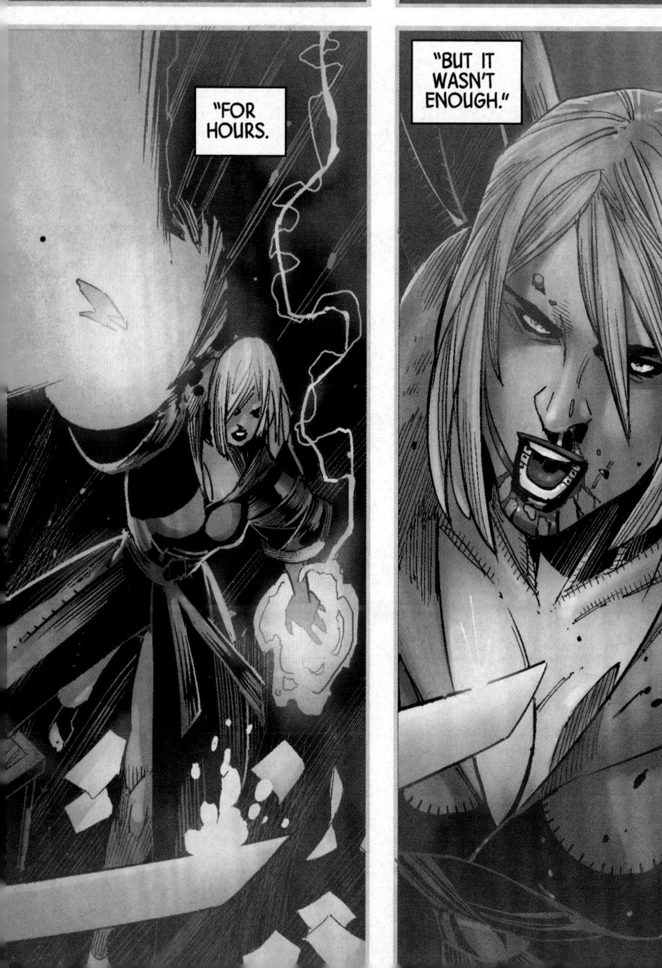
"FOR HOURS.
"BUT IT WASN'T ENOUGH."
THAT'S ALL.
SHE'S BEEN DEAD TOO LONG FOR ME TO GET A CLEARER PICTURE.
YOU DID GOOD.
THIS IS ALREADY MORE THAN I KNEW THIS MORNING. GIVES US SOMETHING TO WORK WITH.

WE'RE DONE IN THERE.
THANK YOU. YOU CAN HAVE YOUR OFFICE BACK NOW.
CANDRA SHOULDN'T BE LAID UP ON THAT SLAB.
PART AND PARCEL OF BEING AN EXTERNAL IS THAT YOU'RE IMMORTAL. YOU DON'T DIE.
V ORLEA
ORENSI
CENTER
SHE'S BEEN AROUND FOR CENTURIES AND HAS MORE ENEMIES THAN I'VE GOT GRAY HAIR.
WHOEVER TOOK HER DOWN...
...IT HAS TO BE SOMEONE POWERFUL.
WITH CANDRA GONE, THAT LEAVES SELENE AS THE LAST OF THE EXTERNALS.
THE LAST?

APPARENTLY.
BUT, EXTERNALS ARE SUPPOSED TO BE TELEPATHICALLY LINKED TO ONE ANOTHER.
SO IT'S POSSIBLE THAT CANDRA SENT A DISTRESS CALL TO SELENE.
I DON'T GET IT...IF YOU THINK SELENE MIGHT KNOW WHO THE KILLER IS, WHY DIDN'T YOU GO TO HER FIRST? WHY BRING ME IN?

BEFORE CANDRA WAS MURDERED, THERE WERE SEVEN OTHER EXTERNALS.
SELENE KILLED *ALL* OF THEM.
NEW OR FORENS CENTER
THAT WAS YEARS AGO.
THOUGHT SHE'D GOTTEN IT OUT OF HER SYSTEM AND THAT SHE AND CANDRA HAD BROKERED SOME SORT OF PEACE.
BUT, GIVEN SELENE'S PAST ACTIONS...
...NOT TO MENTION HER COMPLICATED HISTORY WITH THE X-MEN--
King OF AWESOME
YOU DON'T THINK SHE'D BE COOPERATIVE.
SHE'D SOONER SEPARATE MY HEAD FROM MY BODY THAN TALK TO ME.
BUT YOU THINK SHE DID IT? THAT AFTER ALL THESE YEARS, SELENE DECIDED TO TAKE OUT THE ONLY OTHER EXTERNAL?
IT'S POSSIBLE.
I WAS HOPING THAT YOU WOULD HAVE ANSWERED THAT BACK IN THE MORGUE.
LOCK

ONLY WAY TO FIND OUT NOW IS TO ASK HER DIRECTLY.
SHE'S HOLED UP AT THE HELLFIRE CLUB. APPARENTLY DOESN'T LEAVE TOO MUCH THESE DAYS.
BUT, LIKE I SAID...
...SHE WON'T BE TOO HAPPY TO SEE US.
AND SELENE ISN'T ONE TO BE MESSED WITH.
CANDRA WAS POWERFUL, BUT WASN'T HALF WHAT SELENE IS.
HOP ON.
MAYBE I CAN TALK TO HER?
WOMEN IN THIS WORLD SEEM TO *REALLY* LIKE ME.
LET ME WORK A LITTLE OF MY CHARM ON HER.
CHK
CHK
07
SHE ISN'T THE TYPE OF WOMAN YOU CAN JUST BAT YOUR BABY BLUES AT, LONGSHOT.
SHE'D PLUCK THEM RIGHT OUT OF YOUR FACE JUST FOR TRYING.
RHHHHHEEEEEEEEE
WE'RE GOING TO NEED HELP.
HELP FROM WHOM?
DON'T WORRY...
WOOOOSH

HUNTS POINT
THE BRONX.
"...I KNOW A GUY."
YO, MAN.
YOU LOST OR SOMETHIN'?
I'M LOOKING FOR A FRIEND.
MAYBE YOU WANNA GO LOOK SOMEWHERE ELSE.
STREET'S CLOSED TO THE PUBLIC.
I SAID... I'M LOOKING FOR A FRIEND...
...GOES BY THE NAME "THE STREET SCORPION."
GUH...
TELL ME WHERE I CAN FIND HIM.
PLEASE! MY HAND!

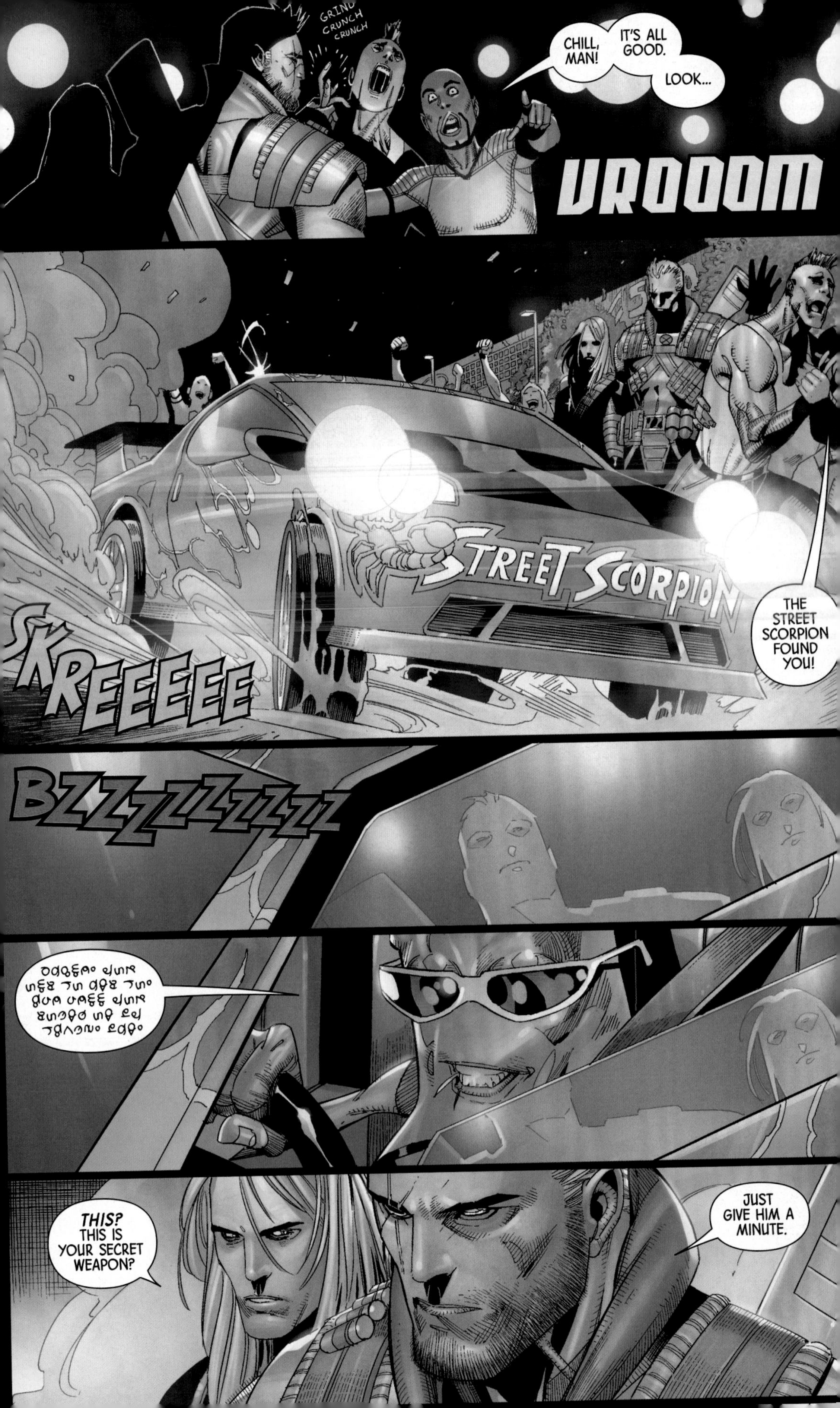
GRIND CRUNCH CRUNCH
CHILL, MAN!
IT'S ALL GOOD.
LOOK...
VROOOM
STREET SCORPION
SKREEEEE
THE STREET SCORPION FOUND YOU!
BZZZZZZZZZ
THIS? THIS IS YOUR SECRET WEAPON?
JUST GIVE HIM A MINUTE.

I NEED YOUR HELP, DOOP.
NEED TO ASK SOMEONE SOME QUESTIONS AND SHE'S NOT GOING TO BE TOO HAPPY ABOUT IT.
THERE'S SOMEONE MESSING WITH THE TIMESTREAM AND SHE MIGHT BE OUR ONLY LEAD TO FINDING OUT WHO.
NEED SOMEONE WITH YOUR SKILLS TO HELP GET US IN THE DOOR.
NO. NO DRIVING INVOLVED.
THIS IS A STEALTH MISSION. YOUR CAR WOULD DRAW TOO MUCH ATTENTION.
NO.
THE MORE TIME WE STAND HERE TALKING ABOUT IT, THE MORE DANGEROUS THE SITUATION GROWS.
ARE YOU IN?
HE'S IN.
I NOTICED.

HELLFIRE CLUB, MANHATTAN.
HALT. WHO GOES?
AT EASE. HE'S WITH US.
THANKS FOR KEEPING AN EYE ON THE PLACE.
KRAKOOM
THIS IS THE TEAM YOU'VE BEEN PUTTING TOGETHER?
YOU ALREADY KNOW LONGSHOT, THE FLOATING GREEN THING IS DOOP.
DOOP, MEET SHATTERSTAR.
DAILY BUGLE
HORROR!
NAME!
Where were you in '92? Rob Speaks!!

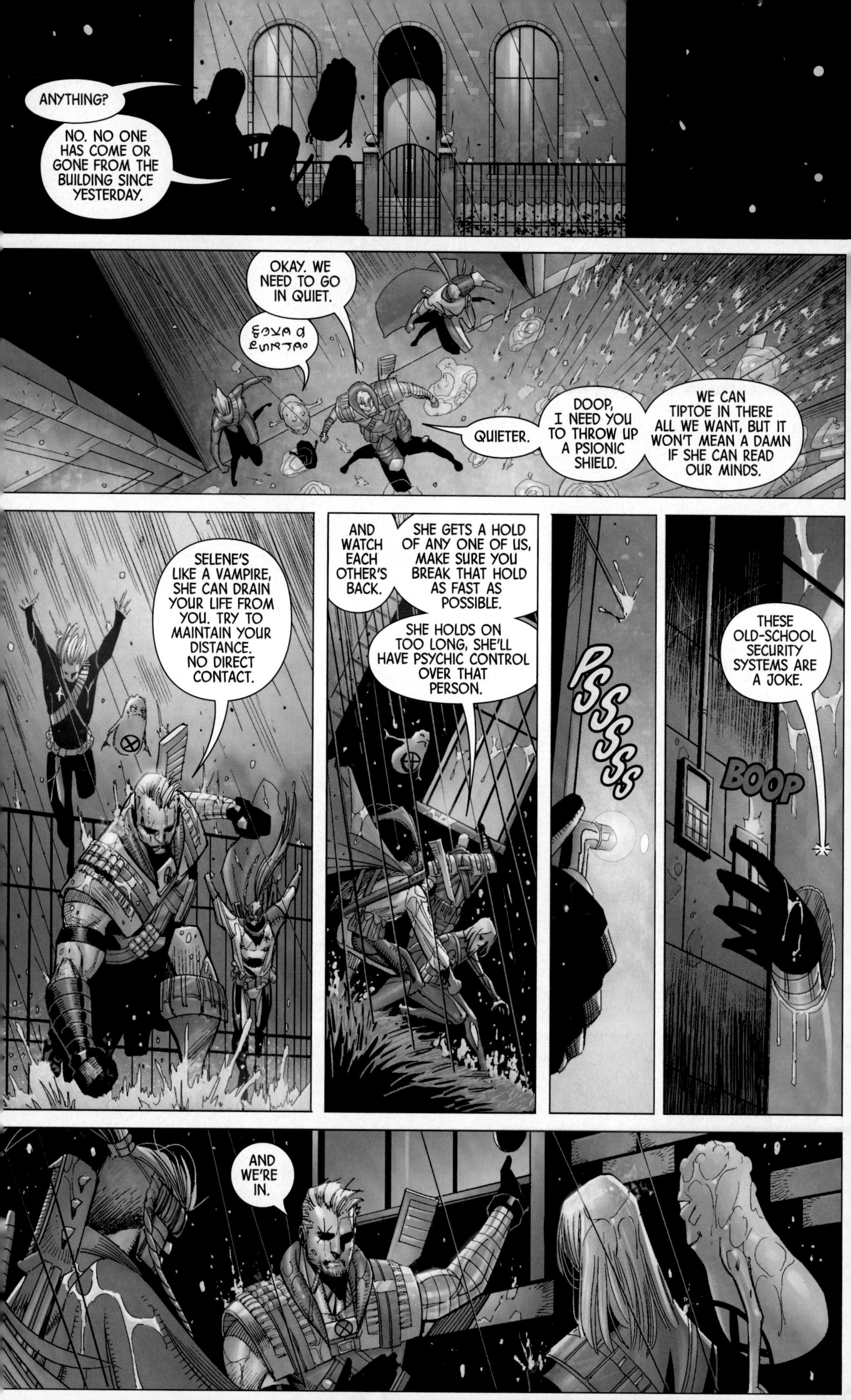
ANYTHING?
NO. NO ONE HAS COME OR GONE FROM THE BUILDING SINCE YESTERDAY.
OKAY. WE NEED TO GO IN QUIET.
QUIETER.
DOOP, I NEED YOU TO THROW UP A PSIONIC SHIELD.
WE CAN TIPTOE IN THERE ALL WE WANT, BUT IT WON'T MEAN A DAMN IF SHE CAN READ OUR MINDS.
SELENE'S LIKE A VAMPIRE, SHE CAN DRAIN YOUR LIFE FROM YOU. TRY TO MAINTAIN YOUR DISTANCE. NO DIRECT CONTACT.
AND WATCH EACH OTHER'S BACK.
SHE GETS A HOLD OF ANY ONE OF US, MAKE SURE YOU BREAK THAT HOLD AS FAST AS POSSIBLE.
SHE HOLDS ON TOO LONG, SHE'LL HAVE PSYCHIC CONTROL OVER THAT PERSON.
PSSSSS
THESE OLD-SCHOOL SECURITY SYSTEMS ARE A JOKE.
BOOP
AND WE'RE IN.

SHUF
CLEAR.
YOU!

SHUMP

WHAT IS--?!?

DID YOU THINK YOU COULD JUST *WALK* INTO MY HOME?

SHATTERSTAR!
EVERYONE PULL BACK!
SHOOOM

THAT YOU COULD SNEAK UP ON ME?

SHOOOM
SHOOOM

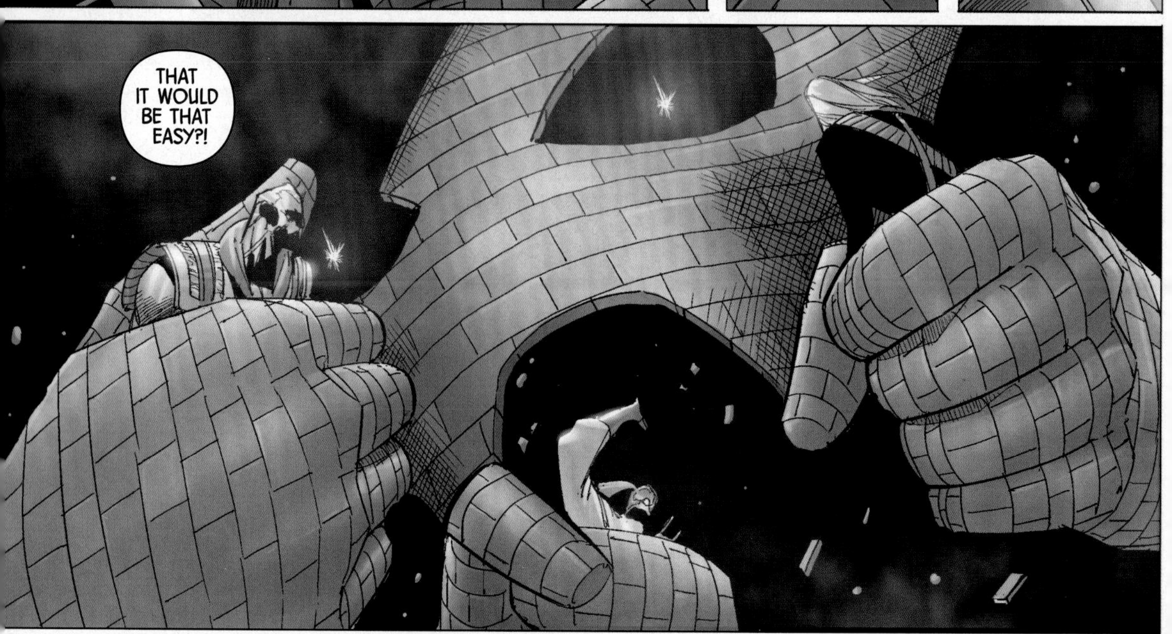
THAT IT WOULD BE THAT EASY?!

I'VE BEEN WAITING...
...EXPECTING YOU.
A LITTLE SURPRISED THAT THE X-MEN WOULD SEND IN THEIR DREGS, THOUGH.
SURELY THEY KNOW THAT I WOULD HAVE EASILY BESTED YOU.
UNFFFF...
LONGSHOT! DON'T LET HER TOUCH YOU!
THANKS FOR THE DISTRACTION, SHATTERSTAR.
CABLE WASN'T KIDDING ABOUT HER TOUCH!
KRAKOOM
CABLE! LOOK OUT!
KATHAK
EVERYONE, FALL IN.

FTOOM
HIT HER FROM ALL SIDES.
CABLE! LISTEN TO ME!
I WILL NOT GO DOWN AS EASILY AS CANDRA!
YOUR PSIONIC SHIELDS MAY HAVE WORKED ON HER, BUT...
...HER POWERS ARE A SHADOW OF MY OWN.
WHEN I TOUCHED SELENE, I COULD SEE...
...IT WASN'T HER. SELENE DIDN'T KILL CANDRA.
FTOOM
FTOOM
YEAH, I'M STARTING TO GET THAT.
SELENE...
WE'RE NOT HERE TO KILL YOU!
LET'S ALL JUST TAKE A BREATH.
OOF!
DO YOU THINK I'M A FOOL?!?
HEAR ME OUT--

CHOP

KATHOOM

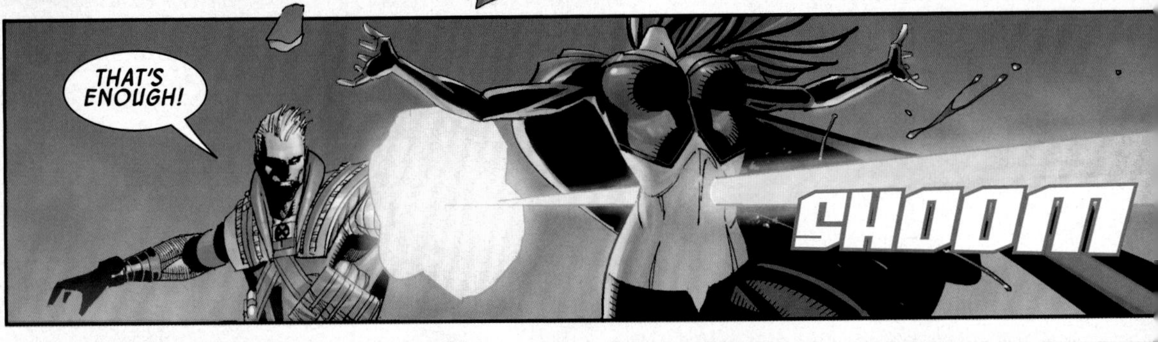
THAT'S ENOUGH!
SHOOM

WE DON'T WANT TO FIGHT YOU, SELENE.
WE'RE HERE TO FIND OUT WHAT HAPPENED TO CANDRA. AND SAVE YOU FROM A SIMILAR FATE.

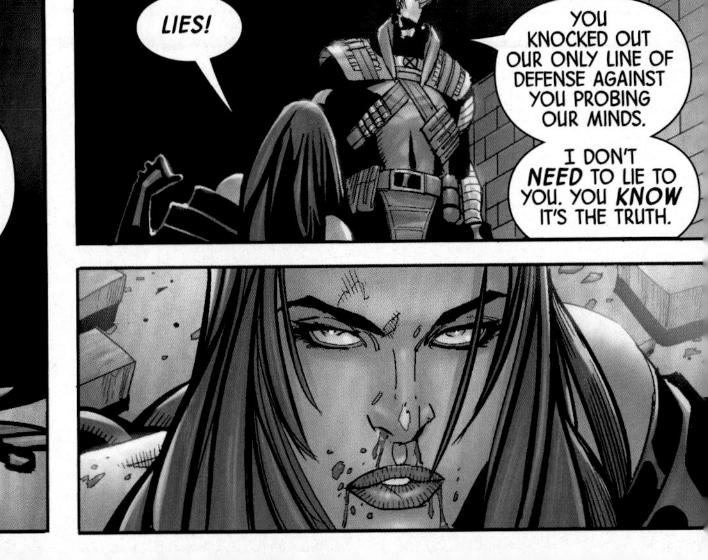
LIES!
YOU KNOCKED OUT OUR ONLY LINE OF DEFENSE AGAINST YOU PROBING OUR MINDS.
I DON'T **NEED** TO LIE TO YOU. YOU **KNOW** IT'S THE TRUTH.

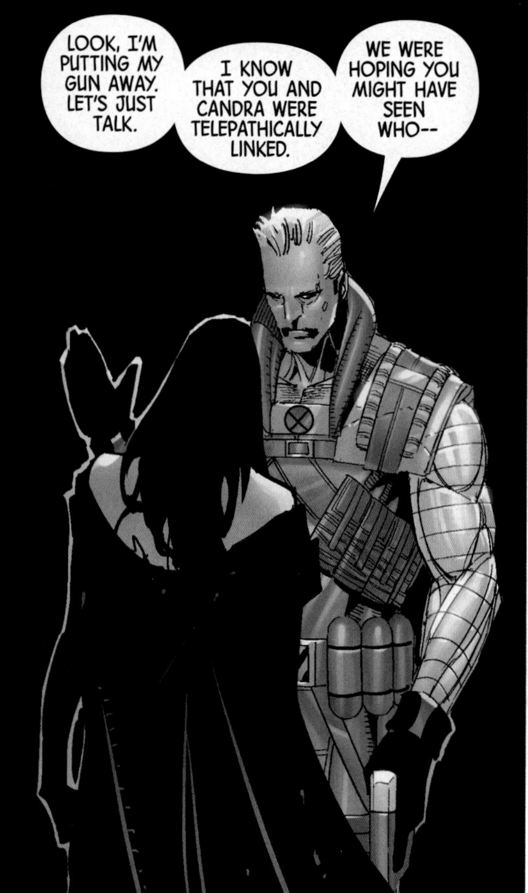
LOOK, I'M PUTTING MY GUN AWAY. LET'S JUST TALK.
I KNOW THAT YOU AND CANDRA WERE TELEPATHICALLY LINKED.
WE WERE HOPING YOU MIGHT HAVE SEEN WHO--

IF I'D SEEN WHO ATTACKED HER, DO YOU THINK I'D BE WASTING MY TIME FIGHTING WITH YOU?
THAT'S *NOT* HOW IT WORKS.
I KNOW ONLY THAT SOMEONE KILLED HER.

KEEP YOUR DISTANCE, CABLE.
LISTEN, IF CANDRA WAS KILLED BECAUSE SHE'S AN EXTERNAL--
I HAVE *NO DOUBT* THAT IS THE CASE.
--THEN IT'S IN YOUR BEST INTEREST TO LET US *HELP* YOU.

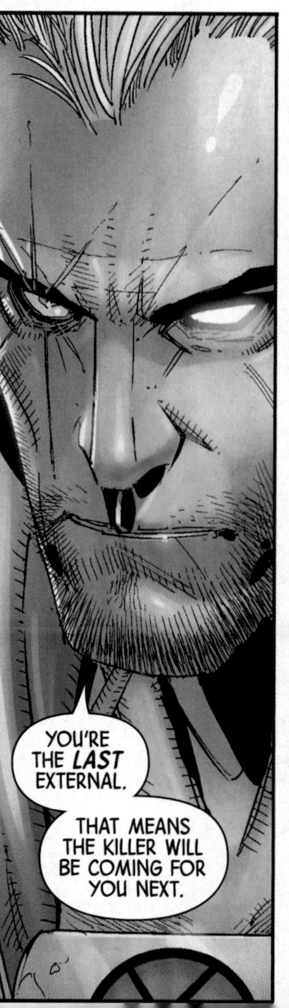
YOU'RE THE *LAST* EXTERNAL.
THAT MEANS THE KILLER WILL BE COMING FOR YOU NEXT.

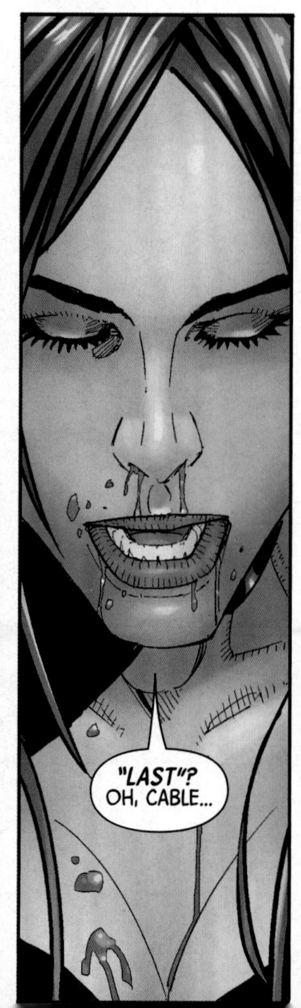
"LAST"? OH, CABLE...

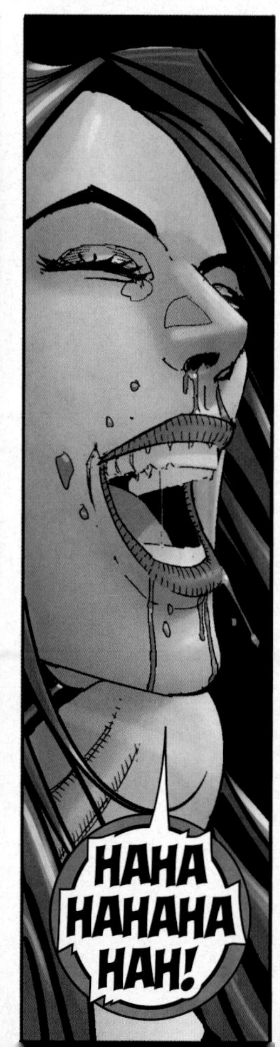
HAHA HAHAHA HAH!

THE EXTERNALS ARE IMMORTAL...
...WE DON'T DIE!
BUT YOU CAN.

HELLFIRE CLUB. MANHATTAN. 13 YEARS AGO.
PUT DOWN THE GUN, CABLE.
AS MUCH AS IT WOULD PLEASE ME TO SNUFF YOU AND YOUR MERRY BAND OF IDIOTS OUT...
...IT'S CLEAR THAT OUR FIGHT IS NOT WITH ONE ANOTHER.
WHICH MEANS THAT MY EXTERNALS AND I HAVE MORE PRESSING CONCERNS TO SEE TO.
WE'LL DO NO SUCH THING, WITCH!
WE'VE COME FOR ANSWERS AND WE SHALL--
SHATTERSTAR. SELENE'S RIGHT.
EVERYONE STAND DOWN. WE'RE LEAVING.
ARE YOU SERIOUS? AFTER SHE JUST--
SHE DIDN'T KILL CANDRA.

SELENE THOUGHT *WE'D* KILLED CANDRA.
TELLS ME THAT SHE KNOWS ABOUT AS MUCH AS WE DO. MAYBE LESS.
NO USE BEATING UP ON THESE CLOWNS IF WE'RE NOT GOING TO GET WHAT WE NEED.
THOUGH, GIVEN YOUR HISTORY, I'M SURPRISED TO SEE NICODEMUS, CRULE AND ABSALOM BY YOUR SIDE, SELENE.
SELENE GAVE YOU THE OPTION TO LEAVE IN ONE PIECE!
BUT YOU HAD TO KEEP PUSHING!
SUITS ME! BEEN WANTING TO WHUP CABLE'S ASS FOR *DECADES.*
CRULE. ABSALOM. *STAND DOWN!*
CABLE, SHOW YOURSELF OUT BEFORE I HAVE A CHANGE OF HEART.
DON'T PUSH IT, SELENE.
IF I THINK FOR A SECOND THAT YOU'RE INVOLVED, I'LL BE BACK.
YOU'D BE WISE TO STAY OUT OF EXTERNAL BUSINESS, CABLE.
WE CAN HANDLE OUR OWN.

LATER...
SO, THIS IS WHERE YOU CALL HOME?
THIS IS ONE OF MY SAFE HOUSES, LONGSHOT.
FEELS MORE LIKE A BUNKER. A FANCY BUNKER.
THAT'S THE POINT. WANT TO MAKE SURE THAT THEY'RE STILL HERE IF I NEED THEM TWO THOUSAND YEARS FROM NOW.
WHAT HAPPENED BACK THERE?
LOADING...

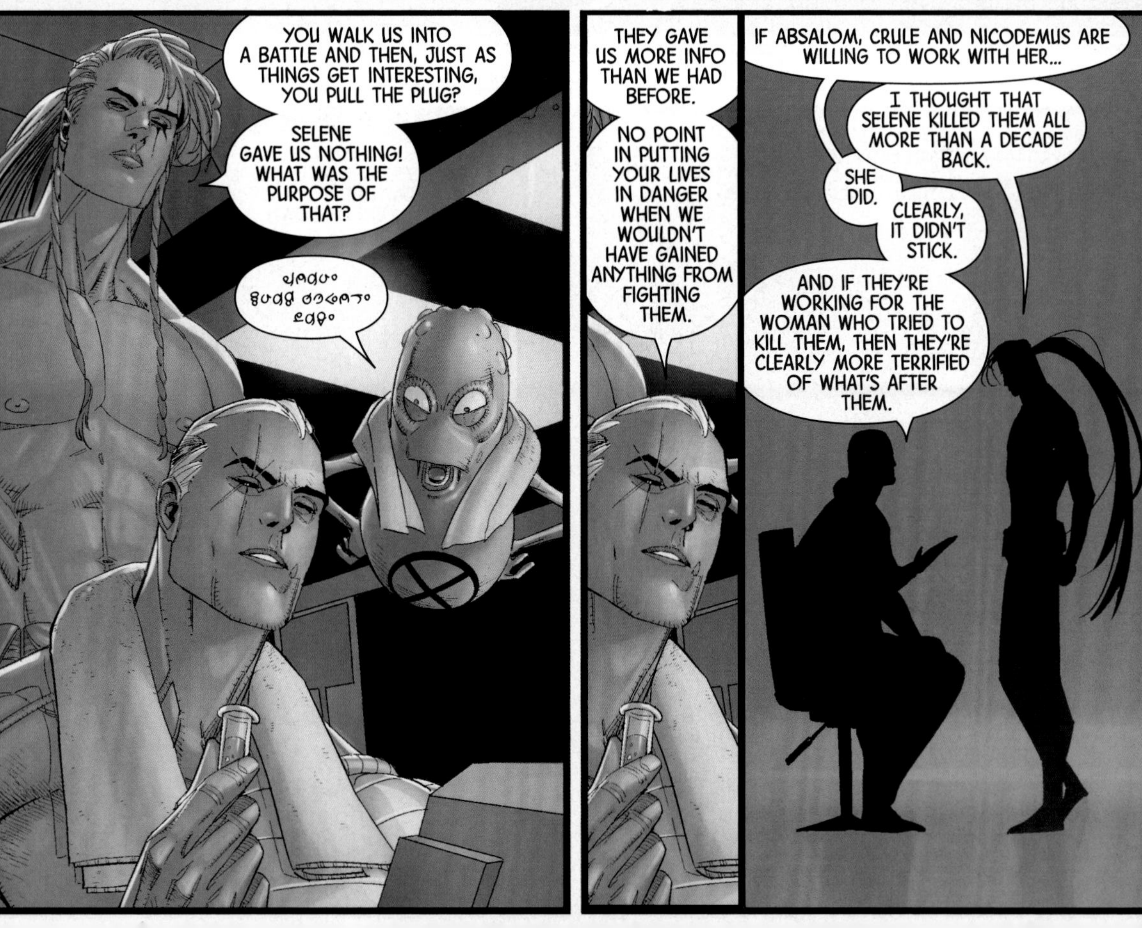
YOU WALK US INTO A BATTLE AND THEN, JUST AS THINGS GET INTERESTING, YOU PULL THE PLUG?
SELENE GAVE US NOTHING! WHAT WAS THE PURPOSE OF THAT?
THEY GAVE US MORE INFO THAN WE HAD BEFORE.
NO POINT IN PUTTING YOUR LIVES IN DANGER WHEN WE WOULDN'T HAVE GAINED ANYTHING FROM FIGHTING THEM.
IF ABSALOM, CRULE AND NICODEMUS ARE WILLING TO WORK WITH HER...
I THOUGHT THAT SELENE KILLED THEM ALL MORE THAN A DECADE BACK.
SHE DID.
CLEARLY, IT DIDN'T STICK.
AND IF THEY'RE WORKING FOR THE WOMAN WHO TRIED TO KILL THEM, THEN THEY'RE CLEARLY MORE TERRIFIED OF WHAT'S AFTER THEM.

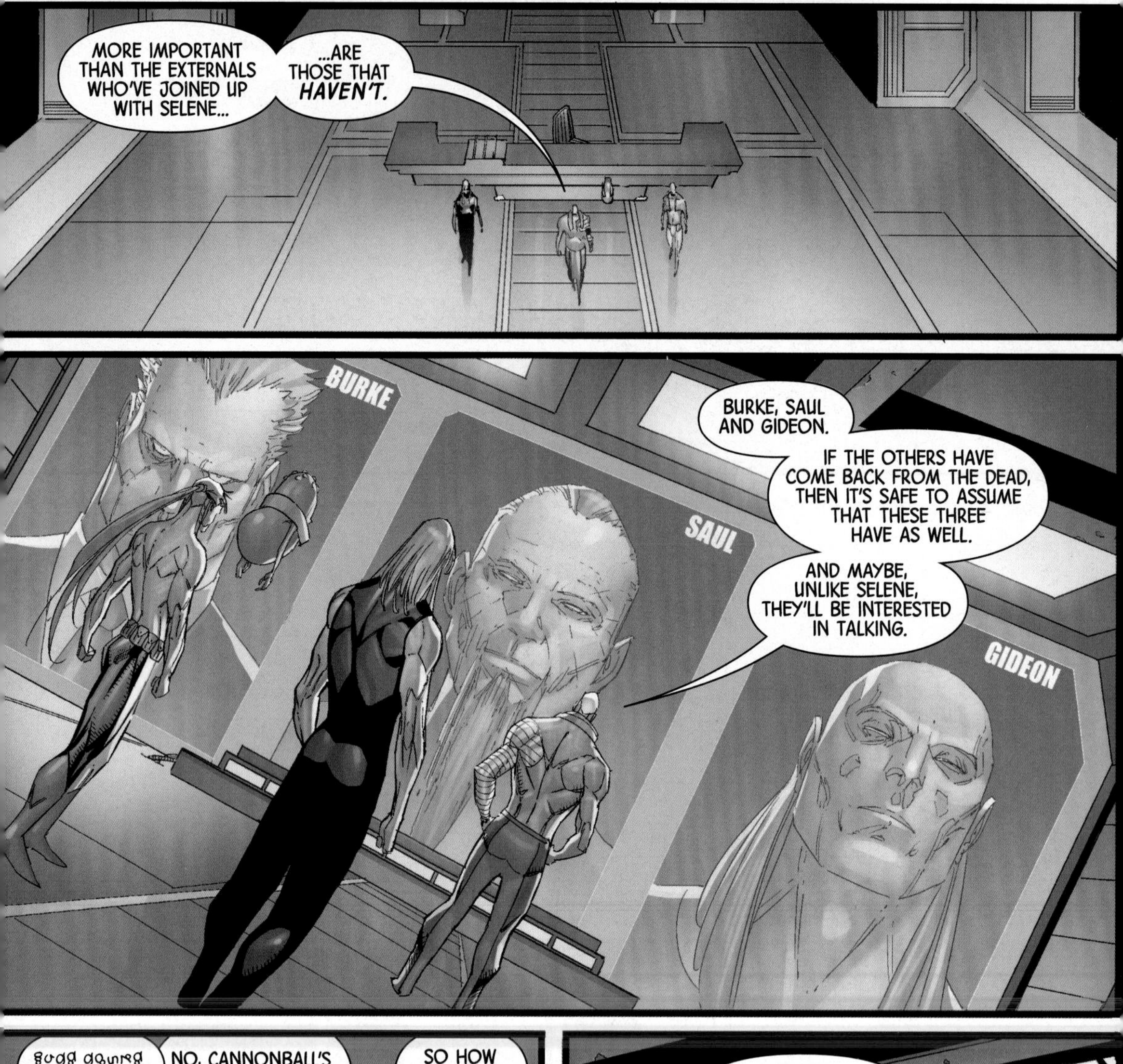
MORE IMPORTANT THAN THE EXTERNALS WHO'VE JOINED UP WITH SELENE...
...ARE THOSE THAT *HAVEN'T.*
BURKE
SAUL
GIDEON
BURKE, SAUL AND GIDEON.
IF THE OTHERS HAVE COME BACK FROM THE DEAD, THEN IT'S SAFE TO ASSUME THAT THESE THREE HAVE AS WELL.
AND MAYBE, UNLIKE SELENE, THEY'LL BE INTERESTED IN TALKING.

NO, CANNONBALL'S NOT AN EXTERNAL. JUST A RUMOR, NOTHING MORE.
SO HOW DO WE PLAY THIS, THEN?
WE'RE GOING TO SPLIT INTO GROUPS. HALF OF US GO AFTER BURKE, THE OTHER HALF SAUL. SEE WHAT THEY KNOW. WHAT THEIR PART IN THIS IS AND WHY THEY'RE NOT WITH SELENE.
BEEN ABLE TO COME UP WITH REPORTS ON BOTH. BURKE WAS LAST SEEN HIDING OUT IN SOME HIPPY COMMUNE IN WASHINGTON, WHILE SAUL IS MOST LIKELY BACK HOME IN MONGOLIA.
GIDEON IS OFF THE GRID.

THAT SAID...
...AFTER SELENE NEARLY TOOK DOWN ALL FOUR OF US ON HER OWN...
...WE'RE GOING TO NEED SOME REINFORCEMENTS.
I'VE GOT A COUPLE CANDIDATES IN MIND.

ATLANTIC OCEAN.
OFF THE COAST OF
GREENLAND.

THIS IS RIDICULOUS.
WHAT ARE WE DOING IN THE MIDDLE OF THE ATLANTIC?
RIGHT NOW, CABLE IS OUT THERE, TRYING TO--
ENOUGH OF YOUR WHINING, ABSALOM.

WHOEVER KILLED CANDRA DID IT BRUTALLY, WHILE SOMEHOW MANAGING TO BLOCK US FROM SEEING WHO THEY ARE.
THAT'S NO EASY FEAT. CANDRA WAS NO EASY PREY.

WE NEED ASSISTANCE.
I'VE BEEN SITTING ON THIS... SECRET WEAPON... FOR MORE THAN A DECADE.
WAITING FOR THE RIGHT TIME TO USE IT.

THAT TIME IS NOW.

STOP THE BOAT.
AAAAAHHHH!
OHGODIT HURTSSOMUCH. ITHURTSITHURTS ITHURTS.
IT'S OKAY, CHILD. WE'RE HERE TO HELP YOU.
WE'RE HERE TO MAKE THE PAIN GO AWAY.

XAVIER INSTITUTE FOR HIGHER LEARNING. THE NEXT DAY.
ARMOR...
OH DANG!
YOU'RE CABLE! AND YOU...YOU'RE DOOP!
I KNOW YOU!
I KNOW YOU, TOO.
OH MY GOD. RIGHT. BECAUSE YOU'RE FROM THE *FUTURE.*
DO WE... DO WE *KNOW* EACH OTHER IN THE FUTURE?
WE DO.
COOL.
WHAT AM I LIKE? IN THE FUTURE, I MEAN.
I CAN'T TELL YOU THAT.
RIGHT, RIGHT. OF COURSE.

CAN YOU AT LEAST TELL ME IF I COME UP WITH A COOLER CODENAME THAN "ARMOR"?
YOU'RE ASKING THE GUY WHO GOES BY "CABLE."
HISAKO, I'M HERE BECAUSE I NEED YOUR HELP.
IN THE FUTURE?
NO. NOW.
I'LL BE HONEST, I DON'T FULLY KNOW WHAT'S HAPPENING, BUT I DO KNOW THAT WE NEED HELP.
AND YOU'RE COMING TO ME? I MEAN...I'M NOT EVEN AN X-MAN YET.
YET.
WAIT...
ARE YOU SAYING THAT I BECOME AN X-MAN?!?
SHHHH...
COOOOOL!

CENTRAL PARK.
MANHATTAN.
ARRRRRGH!
BRAKKA
BRAKKA
SHLIK
SLUCK
UNGGH...
COME ON, YOU MEAT-HEADS!
SHE'S JUST A GIRL! HOW HARD CAN IT...
...BE?
YOU LITTLE--
GUUUUHK...

HELLO, LAURA.
I'VE BEEN WATCHING YOU FIGHT.
WHEN CABLE TOLD ME ABOUT YOU-- A WEAPON, BRED TO KILL--I WAS SKEPTICAL.
WARRIORS ARE TRAINED, NOT CREATED IN A LAB.
WHOMPH
BUT WATCHING YOU FIGHT...I'M IMPRESSED.
I DON'T KNOW YOU.
I'M SHATTERSTAR.
CABLE SENT ME.
DON'T KNOW CABLE.
HE KNOWS YOU.
WE ARE ABOUT TO EMBARK ON A MISSION AND WE NEED SOLDIERS. PEOPLE WILLING TO FIGHT TO SAVE THE FUTURE.
HE ASKS THAT YOU ASSIST US.
WILL YOU?

TONASKET, WASHINGTON.
THAT EVENING.
I DON'T KNOW, DOOP. BURKE'S ONE OF THE EXTERNALS WE KNOW THE LEAST ABOUT. HE'S A PRECOG, BUT MOSTLY KEPT TO THE BACKGROUND. NOT MUCH MORE IS KNOWN--
CABLE!
PLEASE... PLEASE COME OUT FROM THERE. THERE'S NO NEED TO HIDE.
I'VE BEEN EXPECTING YOU.
LOOK, I'VE PUT ON SOME TEA. WE CAN SIT DOWN AND TALK LIKE CIVILIZED HUMAN BEINGS.
WELL, SO MUCH FOR THE ELEMENT OF SURPRISE.
COME. COME.
I RARELY GET GUESTS OUT THIS WAY. THIS IS EXCITING!

HOW DID YOU--
KNOW THAT YOU WERE HIDING OUT IN MY WOODS?
I'M A PRECOG. I'VE KNOWN YOU WERE COMING FOR *DAYS.*
YOU'RE HERE TO ASK IF I KNOW WHO KILLED CANDRA. NOT JUST WHO, BUT WHY AND WHERE...NO... **WHEN** THEY'RE FROM?
HOWEVER, I NEED YOU TO UNDERSTAND SOMETHING...
...I'VE BEEN ALIVE A LONG, LONG TIME. A GOOD PORTION OF THAT TIME, I'VE *ALSO* BEEN DEAD.

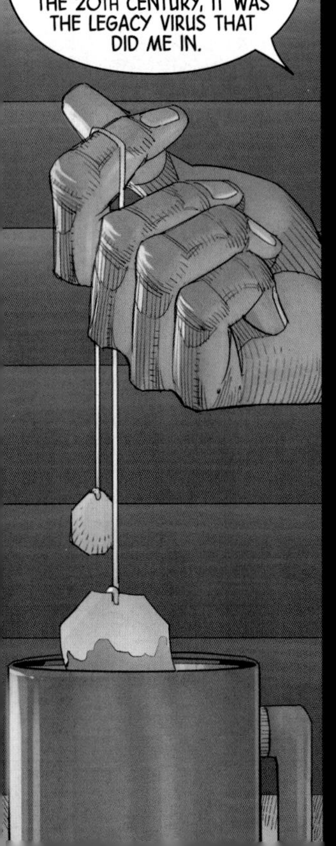
IN THE 17TH CENTURY, I WAS BURNED AT THE STAKE. IN THE 18TH CENTURY, IT WAS THE GUILLOTINE. IN THE 19TH CENTURY, I WAS HANGED. IN THE 20TH CENTURY, IT WAS THE LEGACY VIRUS THAT DID ME IN.

EACH TIME, I PRAYED...HOPED... THAT WOULD BE IT. THE END.
BUT IT NEVER HELD.
YOU *WANT* TO DIE?

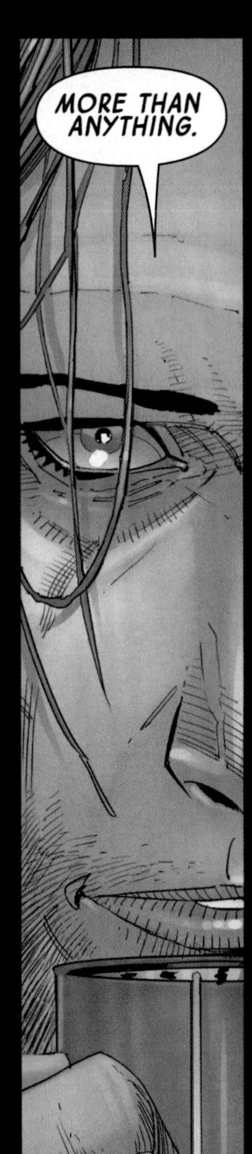
MORE THAN ANYTHING.

BUT YOU GET TO LIVE FOREVER!
THE IDEA OF IT IS FAR REMOVED FROM THE REALITY OF IT. YOUR WHOLE LIFE IS SPENT WATCHING THOSE YOU LOVE PASS AWAY...
I'M READY TO MOVE ON, TO JOIN THEM.
FOR THAT REASON, I'M NOT GOING TO BE ABLE TO HELP YOU.

ORKHON VALLEY, MONGOLIA.
WHILE CABLE AND CREW ENJOY THEIR TEA.
WELL...
...IF THERE WERE ANY DOUBT THAT WE WERE ON THE RIGHT PATH...

WHEN I THINK OF MEN NAMED SAUL, I DON'T GENERALLY THINK OF THEM LIVING IN TEMPLES IN MONGOLIA.
HIS REAL NAME IS GARBHA-HSIEN.
ONE OF THE OLDEST EXTERNALS. HE'D BEEN AROUND FOR ABOUT A THOUSAND YEARS BEFORE SELENE KILLED HIM. THOUGH WITH OTHER EXTERNALS BACK, WHO KNOWS IF HE'S ACTUALLY DEAD.

HE CAN APPARENTLY EMIT ENERGY BLASTS AND... ACCORDING TO HIS FILE... CAN TURN HIMSELF INTO A DRAGON. OR SO I'VE HEARD.
I'VE ALWAYS WANTED TO BATTLE A DRAGON.
OLDER THAN DIRT AND HE CHANGES HIS NAME TO SAUL?
PERHAPS HE WAS TIRED OF HEARING PEOPLE BUTCHER THE PRONUNCIATION OF GARBHA-HSIEN.

REGARDLESS, THESE PEOPLE WERE KILLED WITH A SWORD.
NO SCORCHING OR DRAGON BITES.
WE SHOULD ASSUME THAT OUR KILLER IS COMING FOR SAUL.
THAT HE OR SHE IS INSIDE.
SHOULD WE WAIT? TAKE A LOOK AROUND FIRST, SEE WHAT WE'RE WALKING INTO?

WHERE IS THE FUN IN THAT? LOOKS LIKE X-23 AGREES WITH ME.
I LIKE HER SPIRIT.

KEEP AN EYE OUT, SEE IF ANY OF THE GUARDS ARE STILL BREATHING. MAYBE ONE OF THEM CAN TELL US WHAT THE HELL HAPPENED HERE.
THEY DON'T WORK THAT--
GET THOSE LUCK POWERS OF YOURS TO WORK, THEN.
SNIFF SNIFF
SOMEONE ELSE IS HERE.
SNIKT
SNIKT
WE WARNED YOU TO STAY OUT OF EXTERNAL BUSINESS!
WHY COULDN'T YOU LISTEN?!
THIS TIME, SELENE'S NOT HERE TO STOP US!

SOMEONE HAS FINALLY FIGURED OUT HOW TO KILL US EXTERNALS... FOR GOOD.
AND I CAN'T RISK YOU RUINING THIS.
NOT UNTIL AFTER I'M GONE, AT LEAST.
BURKE, YOU CAN SEE THE FUTURE-- CAN YOU SEE WHO'S DOING THIS?
I NEED YOU TO TELL ME. I CAN MAKE YOU TELL ME.
I'M IMMORTAL, CABLE. YOUR THREATS WON'T WORK.
THERE'S NO PAIN YOU CAN INFLICT UPON ME THAT I HAVEN'T ALREADY SUFFERED.
YOU DON'T EVEN KNOW WHAT THIS PERSON... THESE PEOPLE...ARE TRYING TO DO.
ALL YOU KNOW IS THAT SOMEONE'S HERE, FROM WHERE? THE FUTURE? THE PAST?
YOU DON'T KNOW. YET, HERE YOU ARE, THE SELF-APPOINTED TIME COP.
WE DON'T NEED YOUR HELP.
WE? WHO'S WE? YOU'RE NOT WITH THE OTHER EXTERNALS, SO I ASSUME YOU'RE ON YOUR OWN.
THEY WANT TO STOP IT. I DON'T.
STOP WHAT?!
I CAN'T HELP YOU. AND I'VE DISTRACTED YOU LONG ENOUGH.
YOUR FRIENDS IN MONGOLIA...

"...ARE TOO LATE TO STOP IT, TOO."
SHLIK
ARRRGH!
LONGSHOT! X-23 AND I CAN HANDLE THESE TWO...

SHUK SHUK SHUK SHUK SHUK

...YOU GET INSIDE...
...FIND OUT WHAT THEY'RE KEEPING US FROM.
I CAN'T LEAVE--

GO!
STOP HIM, CRULE!
ON IT!

NO.
NGGGF.

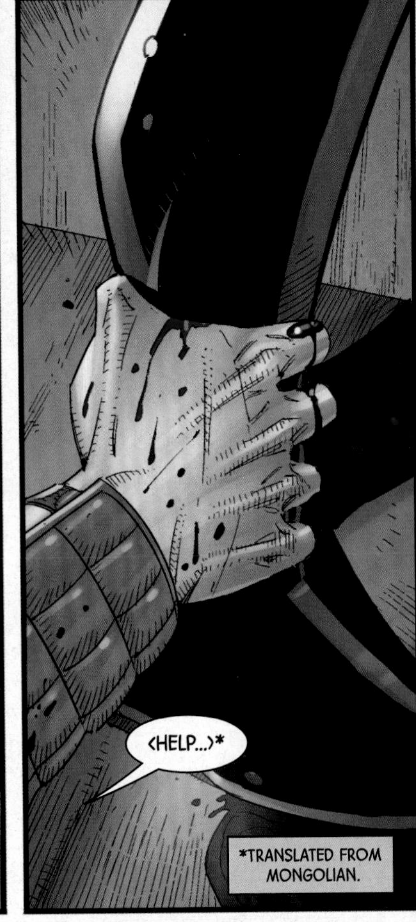

<HELP...>*
*TRANSLATED FROM MONGOLIAN.

<...PLEASE, I'M GOING TO DIE...>
I DON'T UNDERSTAND. I--
WHAT THE HELL IS TAKING THOSE TWO SO LONG?

I'LL BE RIGHT BACK, I PROMISE.
<NO! DON'T GO IN THERE. THE DEVIL IS IN THERE!>

IT CAN'T BE...

SHOOOM
I THOUGHT THAT CABLE WOULD NEVER LEAVE.
YOU DID GOOD.
I DIDN'T GIVE YOU UP.
NOW, MAKE GOOD ON YOUR PROMISE.
SHIIIIK
THANK...
...YOU--

...BLINK?
WHAT HAVE YOU DONE?

152

WHO PULLS THE STRINGS?

SHOOOM
THE X-MEN JUST LET YOU BORROW THE BLACKBIRD WHENEVER YOU WANT?
THEY OWE ME A FEW FAVORS, ARMOR.
DON'T LIKE TO CALL THEM IN, BUT WE'RE IN A RUSH.
HELPS THAT CYCLOPS IS YOUR DAD, I BET.

MUST BE WEIRD, RIGHT? THAT YOU'RE LIKE DECADES OLDER THAN YOUR DAD?
I MEAN...IT IS--ISN'T IT?
YOU HAVE NO IDEA.

ORKHON VALLEY, MONGOLIA. 13 YEARS AGO.

GIVE ME THE SITREP, SHATTERSTAR.
RAN INTO ABSALOM AND CRULE. WE TUSSLED A BIT, BUT THEY RAN BEFORE WE COULD FINISH THEM OFF.
LOOKS LIKE BURKE DIDN'T PUT UP MUCH OF A FIGHT. YOU'VE BARELY A CREASE IN YOUR CLOTHING.

HE MADE US *TEA*.
YEP. TEA AND BISCUITS.
TEA?
AMAZING.

WHAT ABOUT SAUL? DID YOU FIND HIM, LONGSHOT?
HE'S DEAD.

SELENE WAS THERE. WHEN WE FOUND HER...
YOU BELIEVE THAT SHE KILLED SAUL?
I MEAN... I DIDN'T SEE IT...

...BUT IT SURE AS HELL LOOKED LIKE IT.
THERE'S SOMETHING ELSE...

SELENE... SHE HAD BLINK WITH HER.
SHE LOOKED DIFFERENT, BUT...I KNOW HER. FOUGHT ALONGSIDE HER FOR YEARS.*
IT DIDN'T LOOK LIKE SHE RECOGNIZED ME.
THERE WAS SOMETHING... OFF ABOUT HER.
*SEE EXILES! --D!

IS IT POSSIBLE THAT BLINK'S THE ONE WE'RE AFTER?
SHE'S HELPING SELENE? OR MAYBE SELENE'S HELPING HER?

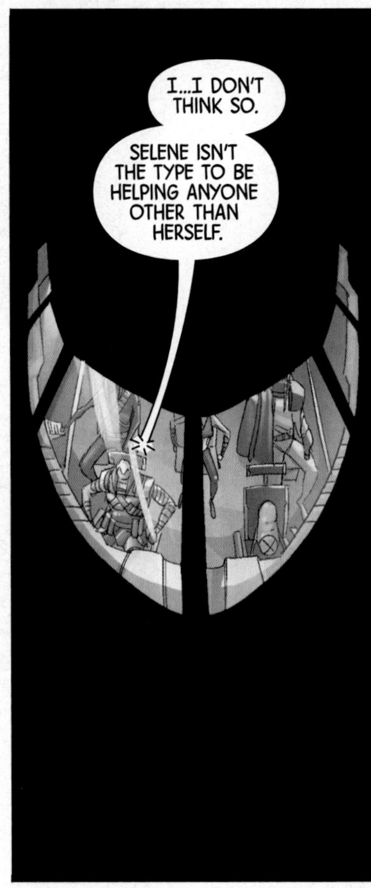
I...I DON'T THINK SO.
SELENE ISN'T THE TYPE TO BE HELPING ANYONE OTHER THAN HERSELF.

NO DISRESPECT-- I'VE SERVED YOU BEFORE AND AM HAPPY TO DO SO AGAIN.
BUT YOU DON'T SEEM TO KNOW MUCH OF WHAT'S GOING ON. SOMEONE'S BACK AND KILLING THE EXTERNALS AND...?
AND WHAT?

MAYBE THIS PERSON IS DOING US A FAVOR?
IT'S NOT AS THOUGH THE EXTERNALS HAVEN'T TRIED WIPING US ALL OUT BEFORE.

IT'S OKAY, DOOP.
YOU'RE RIGHT. WE DON'T KNOW.

WHAT I DO KNOW IS THAT SOMEONE'S KILLING THE EXTERNALS...
...WHICH ISN'T SOMETHING THAT'S SUPPOSED TO BE HAPPENING AT THIS MOMENT IN TIME.
FWOOOSH
AND THAT'S ALL I NEED TO KNOW.
ANY CHANGE TO THE TIMESTREAM, NO MATTER HOW BENEFICIAL IT MIGHT APPEAR, CAN HAVE DEVASTATING CONSEQUENCES DOWN THE LINE.
LIKE THE BUTTERFLY EFFECT. ONE SMALL CHANGE CAN RESULT IN BIGGER CHANGES.
EXACTLY THAT, ARMOR.
I'VE GOT NO LOVE FOR THE EXTERNALS... WOULD BE MORE THAN HAPPY TO SEE THEM ALL ON SLABS...
...BUT IT'S NOT THE WAY THINGS ARE DONE.
SWOOOSH

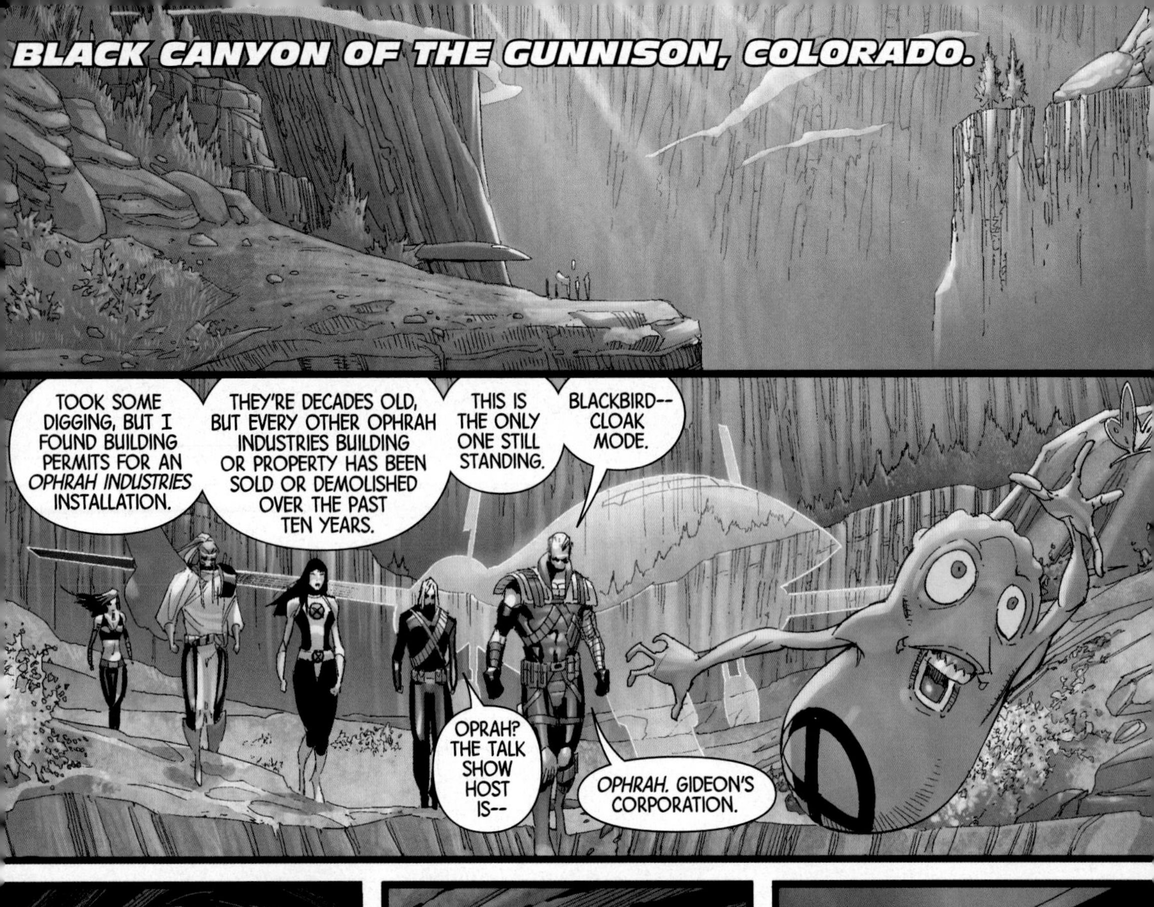

BLACK CANYON OF THE GUNNISON, COLORADO.
TOOK SOME DIGGING, BUT I FOUND BUILDING PERMITS FOR AN *OPHRAH INDUSTRIES* INSTALLATION.
THEY'RE DECADES OLD, BUT EVERY OTHER OPHRAH INDUSTRIES BUILDING OR PROPERTY HAS BEEN SOLD OR DEMOLISHED OVER THE PAST TEN YEARS.
THIS IS THE ONLY ONE STILL STANDING.
BLACKBIRD-- CLOAK MODE.
OPRAH? THE TALK SHOW HOST IS--
OPHRAH. GIDEON'S CORPORATION.

YEAH, WELL, ALL *I* SEE ARE TREES AND GULLIES.
WHERE IS THIS BUILDING YOU SEEK?

HERE.

STEP BACK.
I'M GOING TO BLOW THE--

KA-SHUNK
DOES IT WORRY ANYONE ELSE THAT THE DOOR JUST KINDA OPENED LIKE THAT?
WELCOME.
NATHAN SUMMERS. IT HAS BEEN *SOME TIME*.
DO I KNOW YOU?
MY NAME IS *EVE*. I AM GIDEON'S ASSISTANT.
WE MET SOME YEARS BACK, WHEN I STILL HAD A HUMAN BODY.
MY CONSCIOUSNESS HAS SINCE BEEN PROGRAMMED INTO THIS VESSEL'S A.I.
I'VE BEEN TOLD THAT YOU ARE HERE TO CHECK ON MASTER GIDEON'S CONDITION.
PLEASE FOLLOW ME, I WILL BE HAPPY TO SHOW YOU.
THEY ARE--
QUITE COMFORTABLE, I ASSURE YOU.
THEY'RE TELEPATHS AND TELEKINETICS. VERY POWERFUL INDEED. IT WAS THEY WHO LET US KNOW YOU WERE COMING. AND *WHY*.
REST ASSURED, THEY SIGNED UP WILLINGLY AND THEIR FAMILIES ARE BEING COMPENSATED HANDSOMELY IN EXCHANGE FOR THEIR SERVICE.

AS YOU CAN SEE, GIDEON IS CURRENTLY IN STASIS AND HAS NOT MOVED FROM THIS LOCATION SINCE SELENE TRIED TO END HIS LIFE OVER A DECADE AGO.*
*AS SEEN IN X-FORCE #52. --D!
WHO ELSE HAS BEEN HERE?
YOU ARE THE FIRST TO ENTER THIS COMPOUND IN TEN YEARS.
WHY?
WE ARE NOT GENERALLY OPEN TO VISITORS--
I MEAN-- WHY DID YOU LET US IN?
YOU WOULD HAVE COME IN ANYWAY. IT WAS FORETOLD.
WE THOUGHT IT WOULD BE BETTER TO COOPERATE AS WE HAVE NOTHING TO HIDE.
THEN YOU WON'T MIND IF WE TAKE A LOOK AROUND?

THERE IS NO REASON THAT YOU WOULD NEED TO.
WE HAVE COOPERATED WITH YOU--SHOWN YOU THAT GIDEON IS NOT THE ONE YOU SEEK.
AS YOU KNOW, GIDEON AND *OPHRAH INDUSTRIES* HOLD MANY TRADE SECRETS, AND ALLOWING YOU FREE ACCESS TO THE COMPOUND WOULD COMPROMISE THOSE SECRETS. IT CONFLICTS WITH THE INTERESTS OF OUR INVESTORS.
I HAVEN'T BEEN ABLE TO FIND A SINGLE BUSINESS TRANSACTION OF *OPHRAH'S* WITHIN THE PAST DECADE. WHAT INVESTORS?
AS I SAID: SECRETS.
NOW, IF YOU PLEASE...
WE CAN'T KILL A DEFENSELESS MAN, DOOP.
THAT'S NOT HOW WE--
NOK NOK
SWOOOSH
WHOOOP WHOOOP WHOOOP WHOOOP WHOOOP WHOOOP
WHAT DID YOU DO?
I TOLD YOU NOT TO TOUCH IT.
WHOOOP WHOOOP WHOOOP WHOOOP WHOOOP WHOOOP
"DAMN."

TONASKET, WASHINGTON.

BURKE REALLY WENT ALL IN ON THAT HIPPIE CRAP.

LAST TIME I SAW HIM, HE WAS ALL ABOUT 4,000-DOLLAR TAILORED SUITS AND SHOES THAT COST MORE THAN MY CAR.
ABSALOM, SHOW SOME RESPECT.

ANOTHER ONE OF OUR OWN HAS DIED AND ALL YOU CAN DO IS STAND BACK AND CRACK WISE ON HIS LIFESTYLE CHOICES?

SAME AS SAUL?
IT APPEARS SO, BLINK.
HEART'S BEEN TAKEN.
THOUGH IT DOESN'T LOOK LIKE THERE WAS MUCH OF A STRUGGLE.

I DON'T UNDERSTAND.
WE'RE EXTERNALS... WE HAVE A CONNECTION AND SHOULD BE ABLE TO READ WHEN OTHERS ARE IN DANGER.
WHY IS IT NOT WORKING HERE?
HOW IS THE KILLER BLOCKING IT?
REGARDLESS OF HOW HE'S DOING IT, THIS LEAVES LITTLE QUESTION AS TO WHO THE PERPETRATOR IS.
IF WE CAN REMAIN TOGETHER, FIND HIM, THEN WE SHOULD BE ABLE TO END THIS WITH RELATIVE EASE.
YEAH. I CANNOT WAIT TO RIP HIS HEAD FROM HIS BODY FOR WHAT HE'S DONE TO US.
YES, WE WILL HAVE OUR TURN.
BLINK, WITH ME.
WE'VE GOT NO TIME FOR FUNERALS.
NICODEMUS, LIGHT THE BODIES AND THE CABIN.
WE LEAVE FOR COLORADO IN FIVE MINUTES.
TAP
AS YOU WISH.
FOOOM
"AS EVE HAS ALREADY STATED...

...IT IS TIME FOR YOU TO LEAVE.
YOU HAVE THE ANSWERS THAT YOU NEED.
YOU LEAVE NOW OR YOU DO NOT LEAVE AT ALL.
YOUR CHOICE.
ADAM, IS THIS NECESSARY?
THEY HAVE COME TO HARM GIDEON. OF COURSE THIS IS NECESSARY.
ADAM AND EVE? FOR REAL?
ADAM WAS...IS... GIDEON'S OTHER ASSISTANT. LOOKS LIKE HE GOT A CYBER-UPGRADE AS WELL.
SO, WHAT DO WE DO?
I SAY WE TAKE THEM DOWN. WE ARE WARRIORS. LET US SHOW THEM!
EVERYONE, HOLSTER YOUR WEAPONS!
SNIKT

CABLE...
...IT'S BEEN A LONG TIME.
GIDEON.
SO, WE BATTLE, THEN?
GRRRRRRRRR.

PLEASE, YOU'RE GREATLY OUTMANNED, CABLE.
YOUR TEAM OF...WHAT ARE THESE? X-MEN? X-FACTOR? X-SOMETHING?
THEY DON'T STAND A CHANCE. WALK AWAY.
YOU KNOW I CAN'T DO THAT.
I SHOULD HAVE REALIZED IT WAS YOU ONCE I FOUND OUT THE EXTERNALS WERE INVOLVED.
YOU'RE NOT SUPPOSED TO BE HERE. THE EXTERNALS ARE NOT SUPPOSED TO BE DYING, NOT LIKE THIS.
SAYS WHO?
YOU?
WHY DO *YOU* GET TO DECIDE?
WHY DO YOU GET TO *DICTATE* WHAT IS AND ISN'T FAIR PLAY WHEN IT COMES TO ALTERING TIMELINES?
THE X-MEN CAN SEND ONE OF THEIR CHILDREN 2,000 YEARS INTO THE FUTURE TO SAVE HIM FROM THE TECHNO-ORGANIC VIRUS.
YET, I COME BACK TO STOP A GROUP OF IMMORTALS... ONE OF WHOM, AS YOU AND I *BOTH* KNOW, WILL SOON MAKE MOVES TO WIPE YOUR KIND OUT, AND *THAT*, FOR SOME REASON, IS *NOT ALLOWED?*

SO MANY CONTRADICTIONS.
YOU HAVE NO CLEAR DIRECTIVE, FROM MY POINT OF VIEW.
I CAN'T...WON'T LET YOU MANIPULATE THE PAST.
THAT'S MY ONLY DIRECTIVE.
SO, PUT YOUR HANDS BEHIND YOUR HEAD AND--
GUUUUUUUUUH...
DID YOU NOT SEE THE HALLWAY OF MY MENTAL MILITIA ALL DRESSED IN MATCHING WHITE UNIFORMS?
IT'S LIKE HAVING A MENAGERIE OF CHARLES XAVIERS AND JEAN GREYS AT MY DISPOSAL.
HIGHLY RECOMMENDED, IF YOU EVER GET THE CHANCE.
RIGHT NOW, THEY'RE TURNING ALL YOUR BRAINS INTO OMELETTES.
NFFFFFF...
DOOP!
IF ONLY YOU'D LEFT WHEN YOU HAD THE OPPORTUNITY.
DOOP! THROW UP A SHIELD!

KRAKAK
YOU'RE NOT THE ONLY ONE WITH TRICKS, GIDEON.
WE'VE GOT A DOOP.
PSIONIC SHIELDS AND ALL.
VERY CLEVER.

GIDEON! MASTER, I WILL--
SHRAAAAAK

WELL, THAT'S TRULY A DISAPPOINTMENT.
THESE ROBOTS ARE INTENSELY *EXPENSIVE* TO REPLACE.
IT'S ALL OVER, GIDEON. NO ONE NEEDS TO GET HURT HERE.
I WOULDN'T MIND HURTING HIM A LITTLE BIT.
I BEG TO DIFFER, CABLE.
SNAP
SHUFFFF
I THINK SOME PEOPLE *DO* NEED TO GET HURT.

I BROUGHT THESE HANDSOME SCRAPPERS BACK WITH ME FROM THE FUTURE.
HUMANITY CHANGED A CONSIDERABLE AMOUNT IN THE 3,000 YEARS I WAS ASLEEP...
...BUT IT STILL HASN'T LOST ITS PROPENSITY TOWARD VIOLENCE.
GRAAAK
AND, BY THE WAY...
...THANK YOU FOR THE BLACKBIRD. CERTAINLY MUCH MORE PRACTICAL THAN HOW I'VE BEEN TRAVELING UP UNTIL THIS POINT.
SHUNK

SHOOOM
I JUST NEED YOU TO KEEP THE SHIELD UP UNTIL WE CAN DEFEAT THESE UGLIES, DOOP! WE CAN'T HANDLE THEM *AND* THE TELEPATHS.
KRUNK
OOOOF!
AT LAST, SOME ACTION. I THOUGHT THAT GIDEON WAS GOING TO TALK US TO DEATH.
THIS IS WHAT I CAME FOR.
SHOOOOOM
LONGSHOT!
YOU AND ARMOR GET OUT OF HERE. STOP GIDEON.
WHAT ABOUT THESE--
X-23, SHATTERSTAR AND I CAN HANDLE THEM.
ALL RIGHT, YOU HEARD THE MAN...
I WANT TO STAY AND FIGHT THESE JERKFACES!
KRAK

WELL, WE'VE GOT A BIGGER JERKFACE TO FIGHT, SO LET'S GO.
SHIK SHIK SHIK SHIIIK
KEEP AT IT--WE'RE ALMOST THERE.
SHOOOM
IT'S SEALED. I CAN'T...
STAND BACK.
SHRIIK
KATHOOM
DOOP IS DOWN!
OH...

...CRAP.

153

YEAR 5348.
GASP
GASP GASP
GASP GASP
GASP GASP GASP
GASP GASP
scritch scritch
scritch scritch
GASP GASP GASP
GASP GASP GASP GASP GASP
FSSSST
WELCOME BACK, GIDEON.

YEAR 5352.
I'M SENSING LIFE-FORMS.
YOU'RE MALFUNCTIONING, EVE.
THERE'S NOTHING.
EVERYTHING'S...
...GONE.
YOU WERE SAYING?

YEAR 5361.
WHAT'S THIS?
WHY IS THERE AN *X-MANSION* IN THE MIDDLE OF CENTRAL PARK?
I MUST'VE MISSED THE HOUSEWARMING PARTY.

IT STARTED HERE
LOOK FOR FOOD AND SUPPLIES.
I'M GOING TO SEE WHAT OTHER GOODIES MIGHT BE WAITING FOR US.
CLAP CLAP

OHHHH...
...WHAT HAVE WE HERE?
KRAK

LOOKS LIKE ONE OF CABLE'S TIME-TRAVELING, GUN-TOTING, WHO-KNOWS-WHAT-ELSE ARMS.
I BET IT MAKES A MEAN CUP OF COFFEE, TOO.
IS IT STILL OPERATIONAL?
IF NOT, I'M SURE THERE ARE ENOUGH GADGETS AROUND HERE TO GET IT UP AND RUNNING.
OUR STRUGGLE IS OVER.
WE'RE LEAVING THIS TIME...

NEW ORLEANS.
13 YEARS AGO.
"...AND GOING HOME."
HELLO? WHO'S THERE?
EVENING, CANDRA...
...IT'S BEEN A WHILE.
GIDEON...

BLACK CANYON OF THE GUNNISON, COLORADO.
A.K.A. GIDEON'S SECRET BASE.
TWO DAYS LATER.
ARGGGGH!
DOOP! WE NEED A TK SHIELD ASAP!
WHERE'S DOOP?
SOMEONE WAKE DOOP!
DOOP! WE NEED A SHIELD!

ALL RIGHT, KIDS...
...DOOP'S SHIELD BOUGHT US A MINUTE AT BEST...
SHRAAK
...MAKE IT COUNT.
THWAP THWAP
THWAP
LONGSHOT.
SHLIIIK
SHATTERSTAR.
X-23.
SHIK
THWAK KRAK
ARMOR.

DOOP'S DOWN AGAIN!
YOU DID GOOD, LITTLE BOOGER.
LET'S MOVE OUT.
THE LONGER WE SPEND ON THESE MONSTERS, THE MORE DISTANCE GIDEON'S GOING TO PUT BETWEEN US.
SKREEEEEEE
WHAT IS THAT INFERNAL NOISE?

SHUNK
BREACH DETECTED.
SELF-DESTRUCT INITIATED.
IN 10...
THE DOOR!
NO! I'M NOT DYING IN SOME STUPID MUSTACHE TWIRLER'S DUMB UNDERGROUND BASE!
THWUNK THWUNK
9...
8...
ARMOR! LEAVE THE DOOR, IT'S NOT GOING TO GIVE.
7...
IT'S THE ONLY WAY OUT!
WE'RE NOT GOING TO MAKE IT OUT THAT WAY.
NOT IN TIME.
6...
I NEED YOU TO DO EXACTLY WHAT I SAY, OKAY?
5...
OKAY.
4...

EVERYONE!
FALL IN.
3...
GET
CLOSE.
2...
1...
KABOOOOOM

TONASKET, WASHINGTON.
WOOOOSH
SELENE, STILL LOOKING GOOD AFTER ALL THESE YEARS.
GIDEON...
NICODEMUS, CRULE, ABSALOM...SURPRISED TO SEE YOU THREE WORKING WITH HER AGAIN AFTER WHAT SHE DID TO YOU...
...TO US.
ARE YOU WHELPS REALLY SO WEAK AS TO TURN BACK TO YOUR ABUSER FOR PROTECTION?
EVEN IF THE FOUR OF YOU WERE TO DEFEAT ME, WHAT MAKES YOU THINK THAT SHE WOULDN'T TURN ON YOU AGAIN?
THAT'S THE STANCE YOU'RE GOING TO TAKE?
THAT WE SHOULD JUST SPLIT UP, LET YOU KILL US BECAUSE OF SOMETHING I DID TEN YEARS AGO?

YOU'RE JUST AS MUCH OF A POMPOUS ASS AS I REMEMBER, GIDEON.
I'M GOING TO TAKE GREAT PLEASURE IN KILLING YOU.
AGAIN.
SHRAAAK
YOU'RE NOT JUST FIGHTING ME ANYMORE, DARLING.
YOU'RE ALSO FIGHTING CANDRA, BURKE AND SAUL.
THEIR SPIRITS...THEIR POWERS...ARE NOW MINE.
THAT MEANS I OUTNUMBER YOU--FIVE TO FOUR.
YOUR SPEECHES ARE AS BAD AS YOUR MATH, GIDEON.
THE FIVE OF US WILL HAVE YOUR HEAD FOR WHAT YOU'VE DONE TO THE OTHERS.
DON'T JUST STAND THERE, IDIOTS.
ATTACK!

URK!
SHLIK

ABSALOM, YOU TRAITOR!
BURKE WAS RIGHT. I'M TIRED OF THIS LIFE.

I'VE LIVED LONG ENOUGH AND I JUST WANT TO END IT.
CLEARLY YOU'RE NOT CAPABLE OF GIVING ME WHAT I NEED.
SO, I'VE SIDED WITH THE ONE WHO IS.

THWUMP

TELL ME, SELENE...

...WHY DID YOU STOP ALL THOSE YEARS AGO?
YOU WERE SO CLOSE.
JUST ONE EXTERNAL SHY OF ELIMINATING US ALL.

ARGH!
SHLIK SHLLIK SHLIK
DON'T RUN, NICODEMUS. ACCEPT THE INEVITABLE.
YOU MUST'VE BEEN ABLE TO TASTE IT.
TO FEEL IT.
SHUT. UP.
I CAN'T TAKE ANOTHER WORD OF YOUR--
WITH EACH LIFE, EACH EXTERNAL, I'M THAT MUCH CLOSER TO GODHOOD.
READY TO TAKE WHAT YOU COULDN'T.
I'VE GOT HER, GIDEON!
SELENE!

BLINK... GET US OUT OF HERE.
BLINK
DAMMIT.
I GUESS THAT TWO OUT OF FOUR ISN'T TERRIBLE FOR A DAY'S WORK.
TAKE MY LIFE AND IT WILL BE THREE.
NO.

WE HAD AN AGREEMENT!
I SPY ON SELENE AND THE OTHER EXTERNALS AND YOU END MY SUFFERING.
GET OFF YOUR KNEES.
YOU'RE EMBARRASSING YOURSELF AND ANGERING ME.
I HAVE EVERY INTENTION OF FOLLOWING THROUGH ON MY PROMISE, BUT UNTIL SELENE IS DEFEATED...
...YOU ARE OF USE TO ME.
SHUUUUK

RMMMMMMBL
CLATTER
CLATTER
CLATTER
OH MY GOD...

I DIDN'T KNOW I COULD DO THIS.
SO COOL!
YOU DID GREAT, ARMOR.
YOU CAN POWER DOWN NOW.
DID YOU KNOW I COULD EXTEND MY FORCE FIELD THAT FAR?
I DID.
WITHOUT YOU, WE WOULD HAVE BEEN DEAD.
THANKS.
SHATTERSTAR, STATUS REPORT?
GIDEON TOOK THE BLACKBIRD.
HOW ARE WE SUPPOSED TO GET OUT OF HERE NOW?

WE WALK.
ARE YOU FOR REAL? WE'RE IN THE MIDDLE OF NOWHERE.
YOU'RE NOT WRONG.
CAN'T YOU BODYSLIDE US OUT OF HERE? I THOUGHT THAT WAS A THING YOU DID.

USED TO.
BEEN A WHILE SINCE I'VE BEEN ABLE TO DO THAT.
PRETTY SURE I SAW YOU DO IT RECENTLY.
PAST ME, MAYBE. NOT CURRENT ME.

TIME-TRAVELING MUTANTS ARE IMPOSSIBLE TO KEEP TRACK OF.

SO, HOW ARE WE GOING TO FIND GIDEON?
I'M WORKING ON--

WE'LL BRING YOU TO HIM...

...IF YOU PROMISE ME THAT YOU'LL KILL HIM.

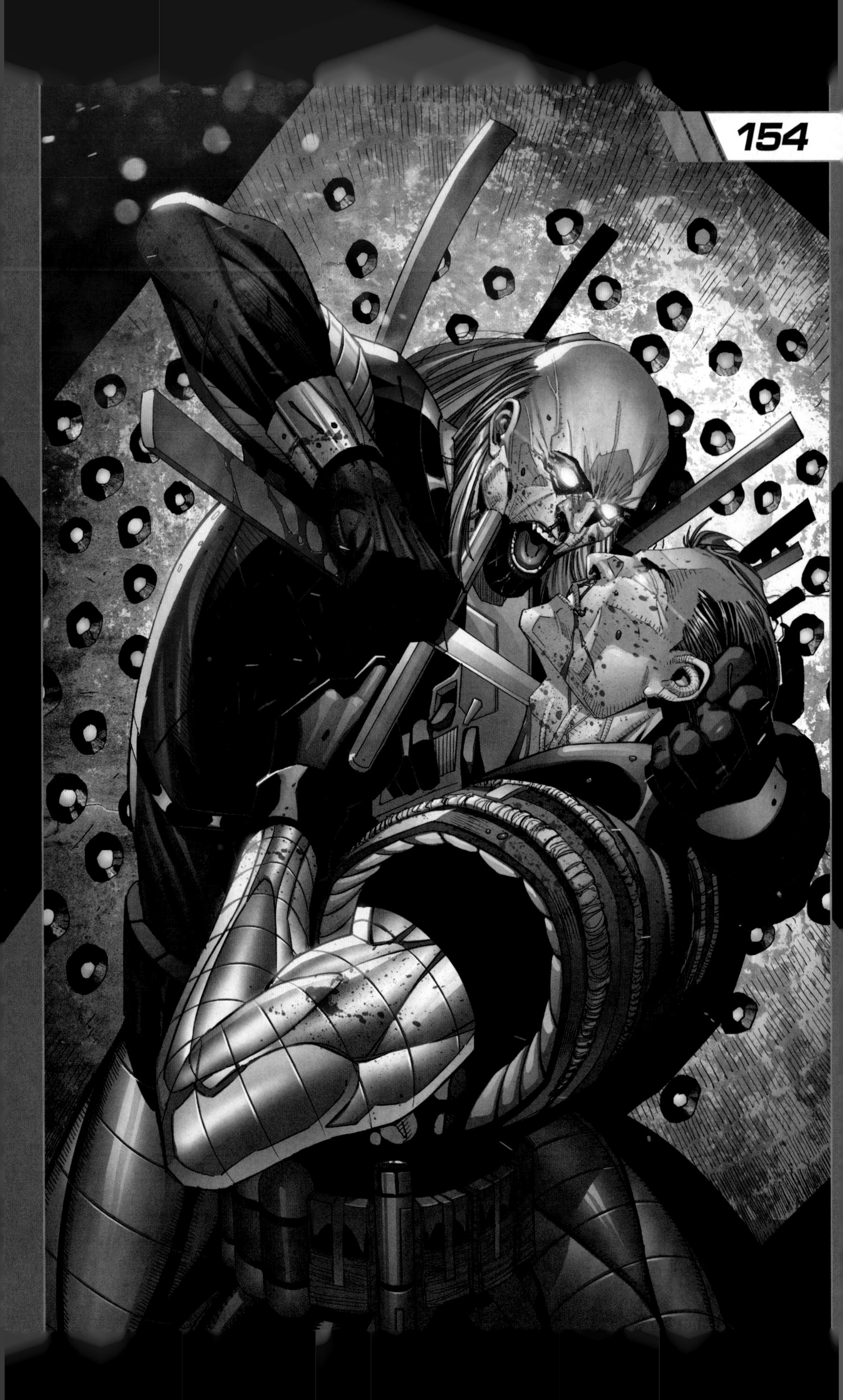
154

BLACK CANYON OF THE GUNNISON, COLORADO. 13 YEARS AGO.
GIDEON'S THE ONE...HE'S THE ONE WHO'S BEEN KILLING ALL THE EXTERNALS...
WE'RE AWARE, SELENE.
YOU NEED TO STOP HIM...TO KILL HIM...
IF HE KILLS ME...
...AND THEN ABSALOM, WHO SEEMS WILLING TO DIE FOR HIM...
...THEN ALL THE EXTERNALS WILL BE DEAD. ALL OF US, EXCEPT FOR HIM.
SOUNDS *ACCEPTABLE* TO ME.
YOU DON'T UNDERSTAND!
IF WE DIE, HE ABSORBS ALL OUR POWER...
...HE WILL BECOME ***UNSTOPPABLE.***

THIS WOMAN WILL SAY ANYTHING TO SAVE HERSELF.
EVEN IF WHAT SHE SAYS IS TRUE, WON'T KILLING GIDEON JUST FUNNEL THE POWER OF THE EXTERNALS INTO SELENE?
PLEASE TELL ME THIS MORON DOESN'T SPEAK FOR ALL OF YOU.
I HAD THE OPPORTUNITY TO DO WHAT GIDEON'S DOING. BUT I STOPPED...
THE POWER WAS TOO MUCH. TOO MUCH FOR ME AND CERTAINLY TOO MUCH FOR GIDEON.
SELENE, I DON'T BELIEVE YOU FOR A MOMENT.
I DON'T KNOW WHY YOU STOPPED, BUT "TOO MUCH POWER" DOESN'T FIT YOUR PROFILE.
YOU'RE ONLY FRIGHTENED BECAUSE SOMEONE BEAT YOU AT YOUR GAME.
I KNOW WHAT YOUR FUTURE PLANS ARE, I KNOW WHO YOU REALLY ARE...
...AND I KNOW WHAT YOU PLAN TO USE BLINK FOR.*
*FOR DETAILS ON WHAT CABLE'S TALKING ABOUT, SEE X-NECROSHA (2009). --DEVASTATING DARREN SHAN
WE'LL HELP YOU...
...ON THE CONDITION THAT YOU RELEASE WHATEVER SORT OF HOLD IT IS YOU HAVE OVER BLINK.

WHAT IS HE TALKING ABOUT?

DEAL.
WAIT! CAN SOMEONE TELL ME WHAT'S GOING ON?

WE'LL DISCUSS IT LATER.
EVERYONE GET READY. IF GIDEON'S POWERED UP LIKE SELENE SAYS, THIS ISN'T GOING TO BE AN EASY FIGHT.
WATCH EACH OTHER'S BACKS.

YOU EXTERNALS STILL CONNECTED?
CAN YOU SENSE WHERE GIDEON IS?
YES.

BLINK, CAN YOU TAKE US TO HIM?
WHAT ARE YOU USING ME FOR, SELENE?

UH... CABLE...?

HE'S FOUND US.

BOOOOOM

GOOD JOB WITH THE SHIELD, ARMOR.
EVERYONE OKAY?
A LITTLE SHAKEN, BUT OTHER THAN THAT...
OOPS.
HOPE THE X-MEN HAVE INSURANCE.
GIDEON...HE LOOKS BIGGER. THAT'S NOT JUST ME, RIGHT?
ENOUGH OF THIS NONSENSE.
IF IT'S A BATTLE YOU SEEK, THEN YOU HAVE FOUND IT.
SHATTERSTAR! X-23! HALT!

FWOOOSH
DON'T PUT YOUR LIFE ON THE LINE FOR SOMEONE WHO'D KILL YOU THE MOMENT THIS IS OVER.
THIS IS EXTERNAL BUSINESS.
BETWEEN ME, ABSALOM AND SELENE.
STEP ASIDE.
WE CAN'T DO THAT.
SHOOOM
CABLE, COME ON...
...I GAVE YOU AN OPPORTUNITY TO WALK AWAY...
YOU SHOULD HAVE TAKEN IT.
NOW!

PLEASE...
KRAK
THWAK
I'VE GOT BURKE'S POWERS OF PRECOGNITION. I CAN SEE WHAT YOU'RE GOING TO DO BEFORE YOU--
SHOOM
GUESSING ABSALOM DIDN'T GET THOSE SAME PRECOG ABILITIES?

WELL PLAYED, CABLE.
BUT ABSALOM WAS NEVER THE THREAT TO YOU.
SHOOOOM
KRAK
I AM.
ATTACK.
DON'T THINK. CLEAR YOUR MINDS AND LET LOOSE.
GIDEON WON'T KNOW WHAT'S COMING IF YOU DON'T OVERTHINK IT.
GRAAAAAAH...

FOOOM
NO MORE PLAYING AROUND.
ALL RIGHT, HE'S DEFINITELY BIGGER. I'M **NOT** CRAZY.
IF I HAVE TO KILL ALL OF YOU TO GET TO SELENE...
I'LL BE FINE, DOOP.
...I WILL.
I SHOULD HAVE KNOWN BETTER THAN TO COME TO YOU FOR HELP, CABLE.
GIDEON WAS RIGHT...
...THIS IS ***EXTERNAL*** BUSINESS.

AH... THERE'S THE SELENE I WAS LOOKING FOR.
THE FIGHTER.
YOU'RE A MORON, GIDEON.
SELENE, NO...
LET HER.
ALL THIS POWER WAS NEVER MEANT TO REST WITH JUST ONE OF US...
...THAT'S WHY I STOPPED!
YOU WON'T BECOME GODLIKE, GIDEON. THE POWER WILL EAT YOU. DESTROY YOU.
BLINK, I NEED YOU TO STICK CLOSE TO ME AND DOOP, OKAY?
WE'RE GOING TO GET OUT OF THIS.
OUR POWERS WERE MEANT TO BE SPLIT ACROSS THE SEVEN OF US. THAT'S HOW IT WILL ALWAYS BE.
I COULD FEEL IT TEARING ME APART AND I KNOW THAT YOU CAN FEEL IT NOW...
FOOOOOOM
LIES. LIES FROM YOUR DAMNED WITCH TONGUE.
SHE'S TELLING THE TRUTH.

I KNOW WHAT THE FUTURE HOLDS. I'VE SEEN IT.
I KNOW HOW THIS PANS OUT.
IT'S NOT IN YOUR FAVOR.
THERE ARE TOO MANY VARIABLES, TOO MANY TIMELINES.
I KNOW YOU, CABLE. I KNOW THAT YOU CAN'T TRACK THEM ALL.

YOU'VE BEEN GONE A LONG TIME, GIDEON. THINGS CHANGE.
SOMETHING THIS BIG, THIS CATACLYSMIC, I'D KNOW.
ONLY THING I'D MISS ARE SMALL CHANGES.
CHANGES THAT HAVE NO CONSEQUENCE. NO MEANING.

WHICH MAKES ME BELIEVE THAT THIS...
...FAILS.
LIES! ALL LIES!
CHUD

I WILL SHOW YOU WHAT REAL CHANGE LOOKS LIKE, CABLE.
I'LL SHOW YOU--
WHAT--?
BLINK

THWUMP
THAT...
...WAS...
...AMAZING!
YOU BEHEADED THE BEAST!
NO!
KRAK
NO! THIS... YOU CAN'T DO THIS!
GIDEON WAS SUPPOSED TO END MY SUFFERING!
HE CAN'T BE--

IS HE...
...IS HE DEAD?
NO. ONLY AN EXTERNAL CAN KILL AN EXTERNAL. AT BEST, WE'VE TEMPORARILY PUT HIM OUT OF COMMISSION.
SELENE'S...
GONE. YEAH.
SHE'S NOT ONE FOR GRATITUDE.
SHOULD WE GO AFTER HER?
NO NEED. WE GOT WHAT WE CAME FOR.

SEE IF THERE ARE ANY SALVAGEABLE CONTAINMENT UNITS IN THE WRECKAGE.
THE SOONER WE CAN GET GIDEON'S BODY ON ICE AND LOCKED AWAY, THE SAFER WE'LL ALL BE.

AND, WHILE YOU'RE AT IT, YOU MIGHT WANT TO FIND SOME RESTRAINTS FOR ABSALOM.
LET'S GET THEM BOTH LOCKED DOWN BEFORE THEY PULL OUT ANY OTHER SURPRISES.

WE'RE ON IT, BOSS.

IF...IF YOU KNEW THAT HE WAS GOING TO FAIL, WHY--?
I DIDN'T.
GIDEON WAS RIGHT. IT'S IMPOSSIBLE FOR ME TO KNOW EVERY POSSIBILITY.
I WAS TRYING TO KEEP HIM DISTRACTED.
DOOP HAD A TK SHIELD UP SO HE COULDN'T READ OUR THOUGHTS.
NEEDED TO GIVE YOU THE OPENING YOU NEEDED.
I JUST WANTED HIM TO STOP...

AND HE DID.
BECAUSE OF YOU.
WITHOUT YOU, IT'S POSSIBLE HE WOULD HAVE KILLED ALL OF US.
THANK YOU.
ALL OF YOU.

BLINK...
...TAKE US HOME.

CABLE SAFE HOUSE.
LOCATION: CLASSIFIED.
SO, WHAT HAPPENS NOW?

NOW I TAKE GIDEON BACK TO THE FUTURE...
...ONE WITH A SUPER-MAX PRISON THAT CAN HOLD HIM.

THANK YOU FOR YOUR SERVICE, SHATTERSTAR.
IT WAS AN HONOR.

YEAH, FOR REAL. THAT WAS FUN.
WELL, NOT FUN. BUT...YOU KNOW...
I DO.
YOU'RE GOING TO MAKE A GREAT X-MAN ONE DAY, HISAKO.

YOU TOO, LAURA.

YOU'RE WELCOME, YOU LITTLE BOOGER.

UNTIL WE MEET AGAIN.
UNTIL THEN, LONGSHOT.

I KNOW ABOUT WHAT YOU'VE BEEN THROUGH, BLINK.
REST ASSURED, YOU'RE IN A BETTER PLACE NOW WITH PEOPLE WHO CARE.
STICK WITH LONGSHOT--HE'LL SEE THAT YOU LAND ON YOUR FEET.
THANKS.

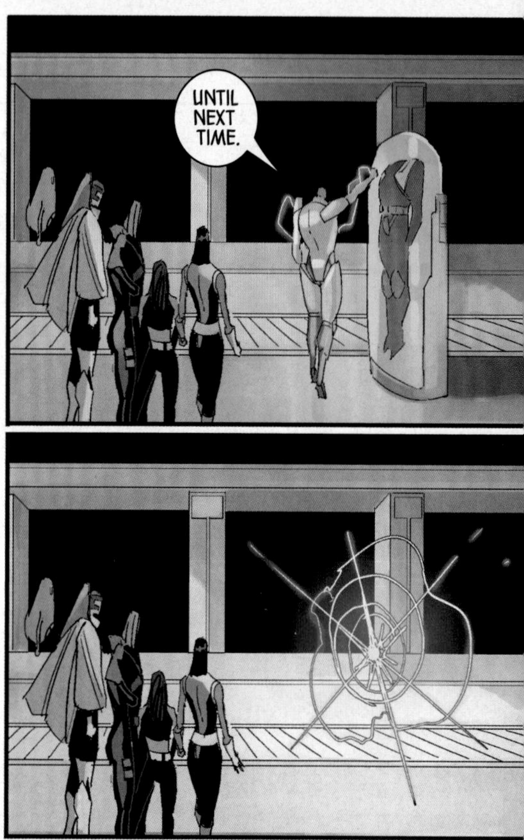
UNTIL NEXT TIME.

SO...
...DOES ANYONE KNOW HOW WE'RE SUPPOSED TO GET HOME FROM HERE?

RIDGE MEADOWS HOSPITAL.
MAPLE RIDGE, BC, CANADA.
CONGRATULATIONS...

...IT'S A BOY.

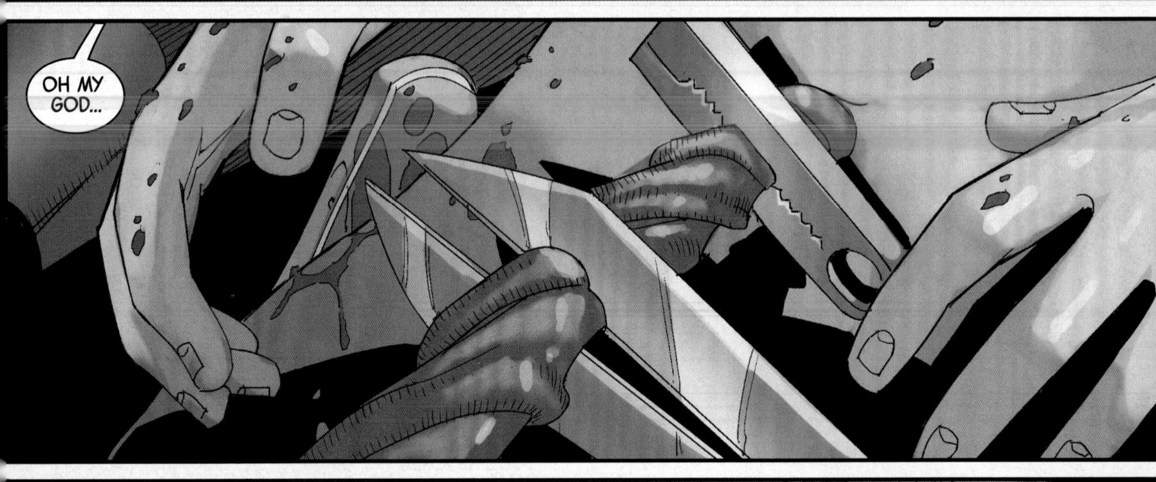
OH MY GOD...

...HE'S BEAUTIFUL.

YOU DID IT, HONEY.
I'M SO PROUD OF YOU.
RENE

RENE
I WAS SO SCARED. IT WAS--
YOU DID GREAT. WE'RE GOING TO BE FINE.

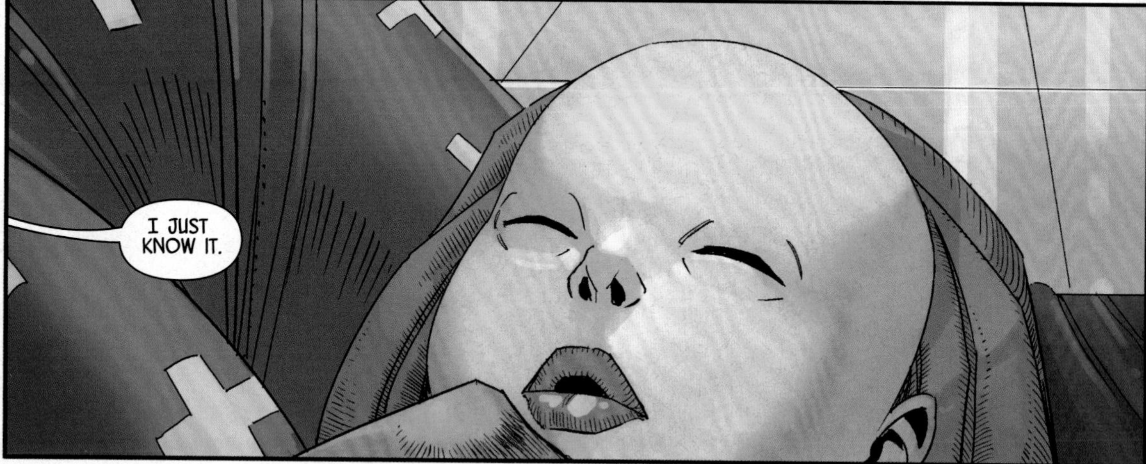
I JUST KNOW IT.

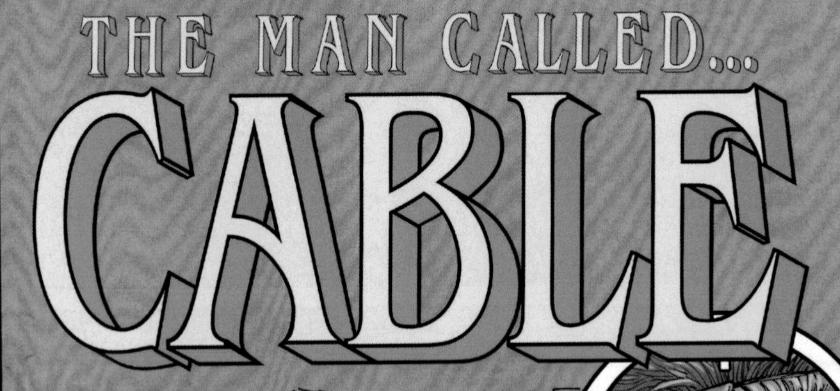

#150 HOMAGE VARIANT BY

CABLE

HOW TO DRAW CABLE
IN SIX EASY STEPS!
BY CHIP "POUCHES" ZDARSKY

Wow! A "sketch variant cover"!
Your first step toward being an artist, the greatest members of society!
Anyway, here's a fun and informative step-by-step guide to drawing CABLE!

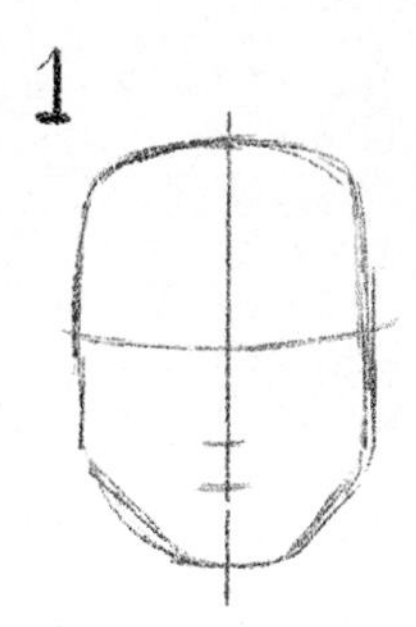

First step is to outline his head. He's got a boxy head, so keep that in mind! Then add guide lines for placement of eyes, nose and mouth!

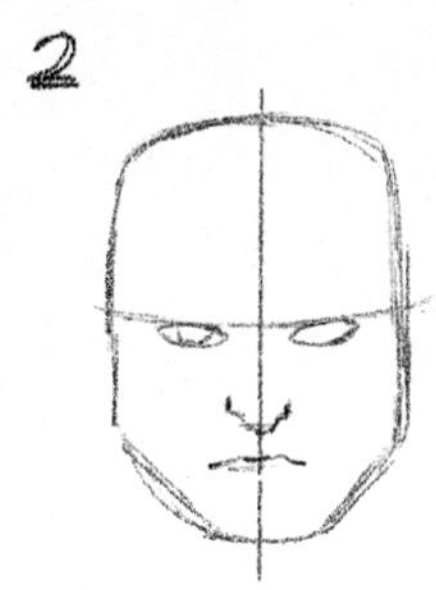

Then start to add features! Eyes roughly one eye apart, mouth slightly wider than his nose. Remember that his one eye is techno-organic with no iris or pupil!

Now for some hair, ears and a thick neck 'cause Cable's a real tough guy, yes he is.

Now, to make him look more like CABLE, add the scars around his one eye and the glow from his other! Looks good, but...I don't know. I feel like plastic surgery in the Marvel Universe must be pretty good, so why scars?

— And if you can get yourself a TECHNO-ORGANIC eye, why not make it look like a real eye so you can blend in better? You know what? I'm gonna redesign Cable, right here, right now! No more of these weird bits! He's going to look like a nice DAD with a good JOB and—

...I have just been notified that I am not to do that.

Add a bunch of details.

Done.

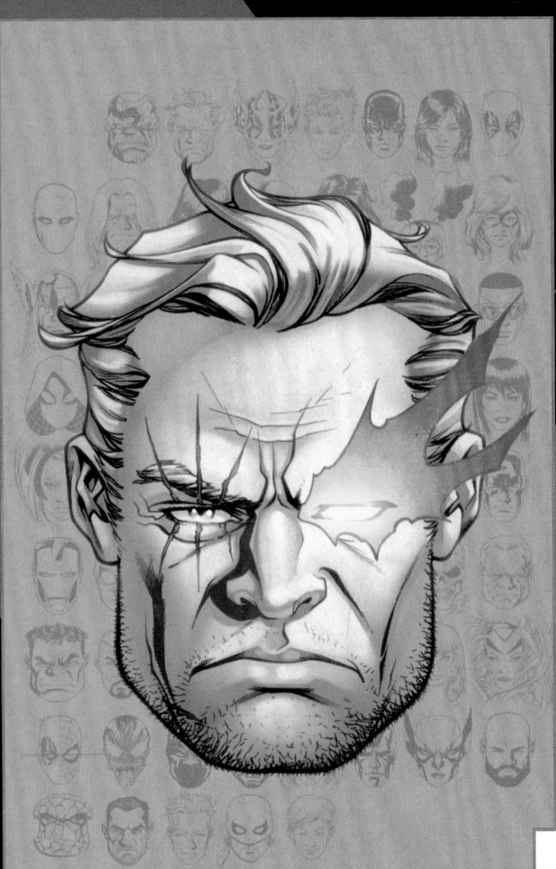

#150 LEGACY HEADSHOT VARIANT
BY **MIKE McKONE**
& **RACHELLE ROSENBERG**

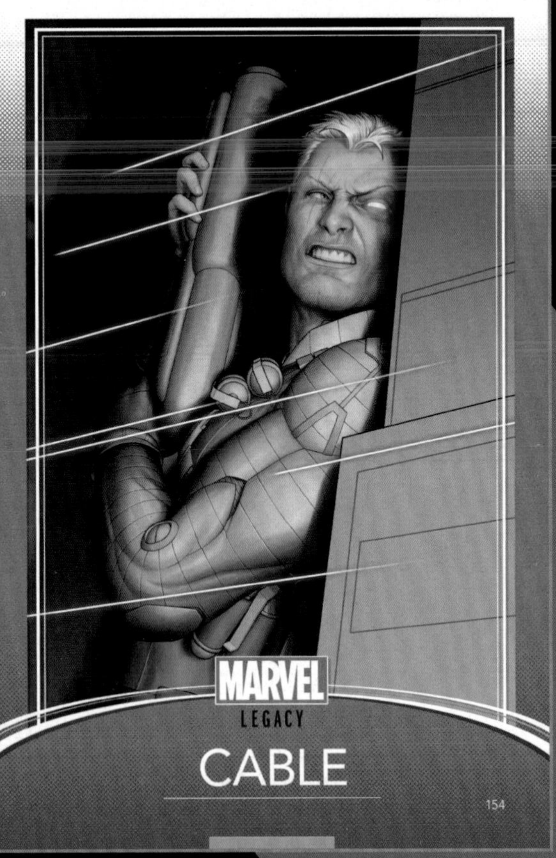

#154 TRADING CARD VARIANT
BY **JOHN TYLER CHRISTOPHER**